WITH

Wait Till I'm Dead

Also by Allen Ginsberg

POETRY

Howl and Other Poems

Kaddish and Other Poems

Empty Mirror: Early Poems

Reality Sandwiches

Angkor Wat

Planet News

Airplane Dreams

The Gates of Wrath:
Rhymed Poems 1948–1952

The Fall of America: Poems
of These States

Iron Horse

First Blues

Mind Breaths: Poems 1972–1977

Plutonian Ode: and Other Poems
1977–1980

Collected Poems 1947–1997

White Shroud Poems: 1980–1985

Cosmopolitan Greetings: Poems
1986–1992

Death and Fame: Last Poems 1993–
1997

PROSE

Indian Journals

The Yage Letters, with William
Burroughs

Allen Verbatim: Lectures on Poetry,
Politics, Consciousness (Gordon Ball,
editor)

Journals: Early Fifties, Early Sixties
(Gordon Ball, editor)

As Ever: The Collected Correspondence
Allen Ginsberg & Neal Cassady
(Barry Gifford, editor)

Composed on the Tongue (Donald
Allen, editor)

Straight Hearts, Delight: Love Poems
and Selected Letters 1947–1980, with
Peter Orlovsky (Winston Leyland,
editor)

Howl, Original Draft Facsimile,
Fully Annotated (Barry Miles, editor)

Journals: Mid-Fifties (1954–1958)

The Book of Martyrdom and Artifice
(Bill Morgan, editor)

The Letters of Allen Ginsberg (Bill
Morgan, editor)

Spontaneous Mind: Selected
Interviews (David Carter, editor)

Family Business (Michael
Schumacher, editor)

Jack Kerouac and Allen Ginsberg:
The Letters (Bill Morgan and David
Stanford, editors)

The Selected Letters of Allen Ginsberg
and Gary Snyder (Bill Morgan,
editor)

Deliberate Prose: Selected Essays
1952–1995 (Bill Morgan, editor)

The Essential Ginsberg (Michael
Schumacher, editor)

I Greet You at the Beginning
of a Great Career: The Selected
Correspondence of Lawrence
Ferlinghetti and Allen Ginsberg (Bill
Morgan, editor)

Wait Till I'm Dead

Uncollected Poems

ALLEN GINSBERG

Edited by Bill Morgan

With a Foreword by Rachel Zucker

GROVE PRESS

New York

First Grove Atlantic hardcover edition: February 2016
First Grove Atlantic paperback edition: February 2017

Published simultaneously in Canada
Printed in the United States of America

FIRST EDITION

ISBN 978-0-8021-2632-0
eISBN 978-0-8021-9020-8

Grove Press
an imprint of Grove Atlantic
154 West 14th Street
New York, NY 10011
Distributed by Publishers Group West
groveatlantic.com

17 18 19 20   10 9 8 7 6 5 4 3 2 1

Contents

1970s

1980s

Rainy night on Union Square, full moon. Want more poems? Wait till I'm dead.

—*August 8, 1990, 3:30 a.m.*

FOREWORD

Allen Ginsberg is dangerous! So, come and get some!
When I first read Allen Ginsberg's poems as a
teenager, they worked on me like a gateway drug.
Leading me deeper and deeper into a life of poetry,
Ginsberg's poems woke me up and whet a poetic
appetite I've spent years trying to satisfy. I saw the world
differently after reading "Howl," "Kaddish," "Sunflower
Sutra," and "America." Language became clamorous
and mystical in my brain, words delicious and unwieldy
on my tongue.

Reading Ginsberg gave me the chutzpah to
complain to the chair of my high school English
department that there wasn't enough poetry on
the syllabus. The chair shrewdly offered to give
me poetry on the side—as much poetry as I could
manage. The poets he proffered—Elizabeth Bishop,
Marianne Moore, Wallace Stevens—sounded tame or
impregnable to my adolescent ears. The chair gave me
Sylvia Plath, but even Plath failed to turn me on (then),
failed to bother me the way Ginsberg did, the way I
wanted poetry to bother me. No, no, no! I wanted
POETRY!: disruption, danger, mind-blowing, dirty-
talking, proselytizing prophecy! I wanted the kind of
Talmudic Beat-babble queer broken-guitar-Bob-Dylan

American song that only ALLEN GINSBERG had the nerve to sing!

This is not to say that my adoration for Ginsberg was monogamous. Far from it! Loving Ginsberg led me into all sorts of wondrous affairs. Having read Ginsberg, I fell easily in love with Walt Whitman who made perfect anachronistic sense to me *after* Ginsberg. I fell hard for Adrienne Rich whose diction, cadence, and density of language were unlike Ginsberg's but whose passion and social activism were inherent to what I expected from poetry (from reading Ginsberg).

Throughout high school, college, graduate school, and beyond, Ginsberg led me astray and into fertile adventures. I never would have read William Blake if not intrigued by the stories of Ginsberg's visions of him. Ginsberg led me to Anne Waldman and back, eventually, to Plath and Anne Sexton. I spent years following a wild, imagined map of Ginsberg's affiliations and associations. The Ginsberg–Frank O'Hara relationship led me to poets who would sustain me for decades— David Trinidad, Wayne Koestenbaum, James Schuyler, Alice Notley, Bernadette Mayer. Even when months went by without reading one of Ginsberg's poems, I always felt he was there with me and in the poems I was reading, a gorgeous contamination. Returning to Ginsberg's poems was never disappointing. Years later, after countless rereadings, his poems still feel *hot* to me, infectious, infected, propelling. His poems invite me to keep writing, to write longer, to write messier, to write more authentically, with more ego and more humility, with everything I have and about everything I am.

My conception of poetry is inspired and ineluctably bound up in my (mis)understandings of Ginsberg's work and life. I embrace a libidinous, expansive, socially aware poetics of opposition and love. It took years for the word "poet" to engender a mental image of someone who looked like me—a mother-writer, her young children in the next room or in the same room or climbing all over her. But I think that because my earliest "poet" chimera was *not* a consumptive poet alone in a dank room with a bit of candle but was, rather, a delirious, bearded, smiling, ranting man, a shy but outspoken Jewish bard, always in the *midst* and *among*—this made me feel that I, too, could be a poet!

For years I felt afraid of Sylvia Plath and Anne Sexton, distant from Elizabeth Bishop and Marianne Moore, and even if I liked some of their poems, I felt ignored (or reviled) by writers like T. S. Eliot, Ezra Pound, Wallace Stevens, William Carlos Williams, and Robert Lowell. But Allen was a good mother to me. He invited me into the kitchen of poetry and made me a sandwich. He offered a messy, imperfect, inclusive, exuberant, erotic (we both like men) kind of poetry that I could share. I didn't end up dropping acid or dropping out or living on an ashram. I never left New York for San Francisco or Boulder. In a way, Ginsberg was a good mother because I didn't feel that I had to (or could) be him (or like him) in order to be worthy, in order to be worth something as a poet or a person. Loving Ginsberg didn't mean I had to be Beat or be Buddhist. Loving Ginsberg meant that I had to be very big and very small, mindful and connected.

What a delight it is to read these old-new poems! It's a bit like watching a memorial slide show of someone I loved dearly. How beautiful he was in younger years! How innocent-looking! How wise! One marvels at what has come back into fashion or never went out of fashion, at the images that feel familiar but are, actually, seen for the first time. "Of course!" one thinks. Or, "I never knew!" I'm so grateful for these unearthed poems, for the *moreness* of them, which is not just memory but new connection, new discovery. I love Ginsberg's fearsome prolificity, but the massiveness of his published oeuvre makes it difficult to get a sense of Ginsberg's development across time. What a pleasure it is to journey through this substantial (but manageable) temporal road trip of a collection and watch Ginsberg break (through) lines like "Ready are we to meet the challenge hurled: / 'To battle, conquer, and rebuild the world.'" Ginsberg knows, early on, that his throat "was tight, as if to choke / My tongue from talk; though in my ear / The bawdy brawl was ringing clear." We get to hear Ginsberg start singing. We see him "wake to see the world go wild" as he writes his "own physical eternity."

I love the tonal range of this collection, which includes euphoric lines like "I am Bard to my own nature nameless as the very Vast I look at" (from the marvelous poem "After Wales Visitacione July 29 1967") and doleful lines like "Melancholy to sit here middle-aged / with worn sleeve & hairy hand / exposed, alone" (from the sad, cinematic, Hopperesque poem "Cleveland Airport"). I love these poems' inclusion of so many of Ginsberg's friends (as direct collaborators or dedicatees), of Whitman (so present he feels nearly word-made-flesh), of John Ashbery, Frank O'Hara, Kenneth Koch, Bob Creeley, Charles Olson, Amiri Baraka, Gregory Corso, Lawrence Ferlinghetti, Bob Dylan, Gary Snyder, Anne Waldman, Ted Berrigan, Ron Padgett, Susan Sontag, Carl Solomon, and others. I love the way Ginsberg always cares *deeply* about *everything*, but never takes himself too seriously: "And I— / 'Om Om Om' etc— / repeat my prayers / after devouring the *NY Post* / in tears—."

I love the short, haiku-like poems: "Awakened at dawn trying to run away— / Got caught dream / shop-lifting" or the poem "Trungpa Lectures" which reads, in its entirety:

> *Now that bow arrow brush & fan are balanced in the hand*
> *—What about a glass of water?—*
> *Holding my cock to pee, the Atlantic gushes out.*
> *Sitting down to eat, Sun and Moon fill the plate.*

And then there are the mini-epics and the awesome "New York to San Fran," a bird's-eye coast-to-coast view, an ode not only to America but to "vastitude" itself. I'm so glad Bill Morgan included the unabashedly sexual "[Poem]" that begins "Bebbe put me on your lap . . ." alongside the sweet birthday poem to seventy-seven-year-old Marianne Moore. The personal, the political, the physical, and the spiritual—it is the tangle of these life forces, an awareness that these are not even, ever separable, that is quintessential Ginsberg.

I am struck (but not, happily, struck dumb) by the alarming timeliness of this collection, which decries police violence, racism, class oppression, and the prison industrial system: "Crazy cars roam the landscape lonesome scared of your police"; "freedom of speech / I'm an average citizen / scared of the cops"; "What divine congressional investigation will ever undo / all these decades of calumny, injustice, / brainwash, jail?"; "Remember pain suffering you caused others Power Head! / Stop & Frisk laws on your deathbed conscience!" This collection reminds us that we are still, too often, "unsuspecting mortals poisoning their air"; that our news isn't new.

I laughed out loud at the very first poem in this collection. Written the same year my mother was born, I had no idea who Gordon Canfield was (until I read the notes) but was startled by how current the poem feels as we approach the 2016 election. Later the same day my son asked me what I'd do if Donald Trump was elected (I fervently hope that seventy-three years from now no one will know who Trump was). "What would I do?" I asked. "Yeah," said my son. What was he expecting me to say, that we'd move to Canada? That I'd stop everything and—"Mom," my son said, "Trump said a woman nursing her baby is disgusting!" I thought of Ginsberg. "I guess I'll eviscerate Trump in a poem?"

Ginsberg reminds me to write with my friends (even the dead ones), even poets I never met (like Ginsberg). He reminds me to have fun, to be serious, to be angry. He reminds me to meditate under the clouds, to give our crooked politicians a what-for, to wonder why the "White / bankers, politicians, police & armies" still control almost everything. Ginsberg reminds me to "come back to my body," to fight the "misery . . . created / to drown the joyful chant / of all our souls." Ginsberg's prescient poems didn't "work" in the sense that they didn't end the inequities he railed against. We need these poems now more than ever. This collection reminds me that our war on terror is a war of terror, and, as Ginsberg says, "War is black magic."

In an age so full of fear, so obsessed with quarantine, isolation, and self-protection, an age in which educators are instructed to provide trigger warnings to students about potentially disturbing material in the classroom and our government issues color-coded advisories about our current threat-level, Ginsberg's poems remind us that art *must* infect, contaminate, upset, disturb, question, invade, threaten, and excite. Ginsberg's poems have always done that and continue to do so. They are dangerous. They are fearless. We need them.

—*Rachel Zucker*

Note from the Editor

Gathering all of Allen Ginsberg's poetry into one place is not a new idea by any means. Ginsberg himself considered doing just that in 1960, when he had been publishing his work for little more than a decade. Yet for one reason or another it wasn't until 1984 that his first "collected" edition of poetry was released by Harper & Row. Even at that point it contained little more than half his poetic output, while weighing in at over 800 pages. At the time of his death in 1997 the collected was enlarged to nearly 1,200 pages to accommodate his last published books, but nothing was done to gather Ginsberg's stray poems until now.

More than anything else, Allen Ginsberg was a steady and prolific poet, and his poetry chronicled his busy life. He wrote incessantly for more than fifty years, from the early 1940s until a few days before his death in April 1997. He was extremely generous with his work, often composing poetry on demand, although he disliked the pressure that put him under. In the wee hours of the night he wrote poems that would be sent off in the morning to support a cause or encourage young students to write poetry. Sometimes he would send his first and only copy, so that he didn't even have a complete record himself of all he had written. At times he grew weary of the work and complained that he was overburdened, but the complaint often took the shape of a poem itself. Once he wrote back to one of his solicitors, "Want more poems? Wait till I'm dead," and from that note comes the title of this book.

There were hundreds of poems composed and never collected, poems spanning the broad range of his life and career. Ginsberg loved gathering his works together. He kept copies of his essays, his interviews, his music, and his speeches and organized them in large file cabinets in his office. I spent most of the 1980s and 1990s helping him organize his journals, press clippings, manuscripts, and correspondence, as well as his enormous photography archive. It was always with the knowledge that some day they would be made available, another example of his generous nature. So it gives me great pleasure to once again work on a project that Allen would have loved — collecting the uncollected.

A Note on the Arrangement of Texts

Ginsberg saw his first collected poems as an autobiography, and so it is with these materials. They should be read as an extension of that and as such they are also in chronological order as much as possible. Virtually everything that Ginsberg created was kept in chronological order from notebooks to fan mail and continuing that practice seems to make sense here too.

In so doing notes have been added where necessary to help place the poetry into the context of Ginsberg's life, not to explain the poems per se. Allen pointed out that his poetic energy was cyclic, that every few years his creative powers would ebb and flow, and this collection also displays "a panorama of valleys and plateaus," as he put it. The reader will be overjoyed to find so many strong, fresh poems that never made it into the collections published during his more fertile periods of inspiration.

A Note on the Selection of Texts

All of Ginsberg's most successful poems were attempts to capture his spontaneous thoughts and insights, what he called "ordinary mind." Composed in that way, in the act of "catching himself thinking," it remained for me only to select the very best examples of his mind at work. This was achieved through careful reading and rereading of texts, whittling the mass down to those poems that best achieved that goal. If the mind was shapely, the art created by that mind would also be shapely was his creed. It also gave this editor the opportunity to reexamine every uncollected poem and select only the best from the entire span of his life without regard to subject matter. So here we follow his creative genius from his earliest political satire at the expense of his local congressman Gordon Canfield through his own "on the road" experiences worldwide.

We conclude with his personal thoughts on mortality as he watched himself and his close friends such as Carl Solomon grow old and die.

Footnotes

Extensive notes, also something much favored by Ginsberg, follow at the end of the book so as not to interrupt the texts. The notes will aid in placing the poems into the context of their contemporary worlds. Ginsberg often quoted Heraclitus by saying "You can't step into the same river twice," here meaning that with the passage of time memory fades, while history and meaning evolve. These notes may help put specific references into the context of their times or lead interested readers to additional information. Younger readers may not recall that Richard Nixon was vice president of the United States twenty years before Watergate, for instance. A note explaining the importance of the Dasaswamedh Ghat to Ginsberg's development of a philosophy of life or why he sometimes referred to himself as the King of May might also save a lot of electronic trips to planet Google. Some notes might reveal the circumstances that led him to write particular poems too. I find it interesting to know his poem "The World's an Illusion" was written for high school students in New Jersey in 1971. Further notes acknowledge the original publication data for many poems, if and when they are known.

Within the texts of *Collected Poems*, Ginsberg made some alterations to previously published work. Not having Ginsberg here as the final arbiter, I have not made changes to either the texts or the layouts of the poetry. Some typographical errors and an occasional misspelling have been corrected whenever these errors seemed unintentional.

—*Bill Morgan*

Wait Till I'm Dead

1940s

Rep Gordon Canfield
(Mine Own Dear Congressman)

Canfield votes like a
Typical politician,
Guided strictly by
November Intuition.
For Canfield is
But half a man—
The other half
Republican.

—New Jersey, ca. Fall 1942

Published in: *Columbia Jester,* vol. 43, no. 1 (October 1943), p. 10.

[Poem]

We leave the youthful pennants and the books,
Discard the little compasses and rulers,
We open up our eyes and test our souls,
Prepare ourselves to wield more mighty tools.

Abandon dusty tales of history,
Of good King Arthur's Knights and Kubla Khan,
We wake, and enter now the world to find
A living tumult in the struggle of man.

For these are giant times, and history
Is fashioned as the minutes burn away.
Buildings of old beliefs are being bombed
And rotted walls are crumbling down today.
Ready are we to meet the challenge hurled:
"To battle, conquer, and rebuild the world."

—*New Jersey, ca. 1943*

Published in: *Senior Mirror* (June 1943), p. 63.

A Night in the Village
(With Edgar Allen Ginsberg)

In Greenwich Village, night had come.
The darkened alleyways were dumb —
The only voices we could hear
Were lonely echoes, sounding clear
From basement bars, where reddish light
Obscenely sweated in the night,
Where neons called to passers-by
"Enter, drink, and dream a lie,
Escape the street's reality,
Drink gin and immortality."

I smiled to my comrades two:
We found a door and entered through;
We stumbled to a smokey brawl,
Reality fled beyond recall.
We sat down jesting, wit in flower,
Disputed wildly, burned the hour;
We drank a river of delight,
While pleasure's flame was kindled bright;
Memory came, and memory flew,
Dreams were lost, and born anew . . .

Suddenly it seemed, I woke —
My throat was tight, as if to choke

My tongue from talk; though in my ear
The bawdy bawl was ringing clear,
Its meaning I no longer guessed;
My heart was thundering in my breast.
I looked up horrified to see
Eternity glaring down at me!
I looked about in wild alarm —
Death met my glance. He raised his arm:
Futility, mirrored everyplace,
Dwelled in every person's face —
In every visage was that taint.
Underneath a woman's paint,
Undisguised by colored lead,
Leered a mocking white Death's head.
Under the lurid light, the room
Was flushed with shame and vivid doom.

Reflected in a whiskey glass,
Fate's yellow eyes were molten brass;
In undertones, beneath a note,
Death spoke out of the singer's throat;
While, staring through a drunkard's eyes,
Fate confounded drinker's lies:
For all the drinks that they had tried,
Death still sat there at their side.
And Death peered with contemptuous calm
From the barman's open palm.
Thus, waiting patiently, alas,
Conferring there, and clinking glass,

And toasting Death, their drinking mate,
Bent Time, Futility, and Fate.

A woman's laughter rent the gloom —
And back came once again the room.

—New York, Spring 1944

Published in: *Columbia Jester,* vol. 43, no. 6 (May 1944), p. 2.

Epitaph for a Suicide

A weary lover
    Once he was,
Who wept as only
    A lover does.

Or laughed as only
    A lover must.
Now his mouth
    Is ringed with dust.

The credit's his —
    He was quite brave,
To shut his loving
    In his grave.

Epitaph for a Poet

This single pleasure
    I have had:
I sang a song
    When I was sad.

But since my lips
    Would rot, in time,
I put my singing
    In a rhyme.

On other lips
    My songs will ring,
Now I am dead
    And must not sing.

—New York, August 20, 1944

"Epitaph for a Suicide" was published in: Allen Ginsberg, *The Book of Martyrdom and Artifice* (DaCapo Press, 2006). "Epitaph for a Poet" was published in: *Columbia Jester,* vol. 43, no. 9 (October 1944), p. 13.

Song

Winds around the beaches blow:
Things being as they are, although
Half clearly understood, and I
Uncurious of mystery;

Such thoughts as once were my despair,
— The frantic sea, the silent air,
The changing moon, the frigid shore —
I find delight me more and more.

I had not dreamed the sea so deep,
The earth so dark; so long my sleep,
I have become another child.
I wake to see the world go wild.

—ca. 1946

Published in: *Columbia Review,* vol. 27, no. 3 (February 1947),
p. 32.

[Poem]

To live and deal with life as if it were a stone.
Time like a turning stone that grinds my bones.
Time is a dog that gnaws my bones
and grinds my soul to sticks and stones

It's not mere time
that pricks my pride;
Just let my bones
Be satisfied.

—May 21, 1949

Published in: James E. B. Breslin, *From Modern to Contemporary.*
(University of Chicago Press, June 1984), p. 88.

Behold! The Swinging Swan

Behold! the swinging swan
Where the geese have gamboled

    Say my oops
    Beat my bones

All my eggs are scrambled.

—1949

Published in: Allen Ginsberg and Jack Kerouac, *Take Care of My Ghost, Ghost* (Ghost Press, ca. June 1977), p. 3.

1950s

Her Engagement

We have to go through the warehouse
to get to the lunchroom —
        and he asked me for a date,
and he told me where we were going,
and he told me what time
        he would pick me up —
what a doll he is.

        We were walking
through the warehouse
        hand in hand
and when we got near
        the loading platform
he held my fingers
        and kissed me

        — we had to hide:
if anybody in Accounting
        knew, the news
would spread like wildfire.

—New York–California, March 30, 1952

Published in: *Voices*, no. 158 (September–December 1955), p. 10.

Hitch-Hiking Key West

I walked for miles
    toward that bedroom
on the starlit highway
    in the lonesome night.

I knock. The bridegroom
    opens the door.
'I've come on the first
    night as due.'

'Farewell, man,'
    his reply.
I go into the house,
    he to the wild.

—ca. December 1953

Published in: *Yugen,* no. 1 ([March 13], 1958), p. 22.

In a Red Bar

I look like someone else
I don't like in the mirror
— a floating city heel,
middleclass con artist,
I need a haircut and look
seedy — in late twenties,
shadows under my mouth,
too informally dressed,
heavy eyebrowed, sadistic,
too mental and lonely.

—ca. 1954

Published in: *Yugen,* no. 1 ([March 13], 1958), p. 23.

[Poem]

What's buzzing
    in my head?
Self loathing? I
    hate myself?
What literary
    abstraction!
Ha! I'll kill
    that fly!

—San Jose, 1954

Published in: *Beatitude,* no. 6 (June [ca. 13] 1959), p. 17.

Thus on a Long Bus Ride

thus on a long bus ride
    my soul woke
arm in arm with a youth:
hours of communion
    warm thighs
shoulders touching
bodies moved together
    as we rode on
dreaming invisibly

—*San Francisco, April 1, 1955*

Published in: *Take Care of My Ghost, Ghost,* (Ghost Press, ca. June 1977), p. 3.

[Poem]

We rode on a lonely bus
    for half a night,
shoulders touching, warmth
    between our thighs,
bodies moved together
    dreaming invisibly.

I longed for a look of secrecy
    with open eyes
— intimacies of New Jersey —
    holding hands
and kissing golden cheeks.

Published in: *Yugen*, no. 1 ([March 13] 1958), p. 22.

[Poem]

There's nobody here
    to talk to.
San Francisco house
    April 12, '55
Slam of Neal's car
    door outside
my shade at twilight.
Great art learned in
    desolation.
Empty another ashtray.

—San Francisco, April 12, 1955

Published in: *Beatitude,* no. 2 (May 16, 1959), p. 5.

On Nixon; Chain Poem
(by Allen Ginsberg, Gregory Corso,
and Jack Kerouac)

Nixon has a pillow in his mouth in the kitchen
Nixon has chickenfeathers coming out of his fly
Nixon's hair is purple like the egg-yolk of a saurian
       reptile
Nixon's ears whistle
Nixon's eyes whip back and forth like taxicabs
Nixon has a soul, the roses of the unborn, alas
Nixon never plays a bongo drum & that's why he's so
       lonely
Nixon is deathified towards two lonely cops
Nixon's head is full of pork
Nixon left his kissing lipstick on his television lensglass
His sweating pissing chin
Nixon wears silk shorts covered with shitscum
Nixon doesn't know Lafcadio [Orlovsky]

—late 1956 – early 1957

Published in: *Bombay Gin,* no. 7 (Summer/Fall [1980] 1979), p. 1.

Dawn

Dawn:
      fatigue
  — white sky
      grey concrete houses
sun rust red —
  coming home to the furnished room
— nervewracking lovetalk.
      I don't *want* her

Stop all fantasy!

     live
in the physical world
  moment to moment

I must write down
      every recurring thought —
  stop every beating second

fire-escape, stoop, stairway,
  door,
      electric light,

desk and bed — weariness —
    drunken sensation
of my own physical eternity.

—ca. Spring 1958 or before

Published in: *Chicago Review,* vol. 12, no. 1 (Spring 1958), p. 11.

A Lion Met America

A Lion met America
On the crossroads in the desert
Two figures
Stared at each other.

America screamed
The Lion roared
They leaped desperately
Knives forks submarines.

The Lion bit the head off America
And loped off to the golden hills
That's all there is to say
About America except
That now she's
Lionshit all over the desert.

—ca. 1959

Published in: *Beetitood [Beatitude],* no. 7 (July 4, 1959), p. 16.

Leave the Bones Behind

Leave the bones behind
they're only bones
leave the mind behind
it's only thoughts
leave the man behind
he cannot live
Save the soul! But
    Soul is ever Safe
       & Sole
Itself Beauty's representative
Lost in accidental form
that'll soon be over with
    when its nose falls off
    and its eyes fall out
and leaves it alone to be itself
    lone in One
       Gold Be.

—October 6, 1959

Published in: *Take Care of My Ghost, Ghost* (Ghost Press, ca. June 1977), p. 8.

The Real Distinguished Thing

(Steps to Unconsciousness under Laughing Gas)

High sentience of my presence in the grand
    harmonious Being
. . . in which The unknowable disharmony
    will now take place
de ja-vu — "I'm back here again" — sensation
    of mechanical illusion relapsing to its
    stupid fate — with banal triumphant
    music — I give up
Glimpse of infinite co-incidental structures
    of horrific Reality risen by mistake and
    left behind in silly realms of Nowhere
    consciousness
vanishing into the closing asshole of the void
    — a Stop Sign whirling & receding to the
    size of an eye in a peephole — gives me
    an ignorant wink & we disappear.

—ca. 1959

Published in: *Damascus Road,* no. 1 (1961), p. 46.

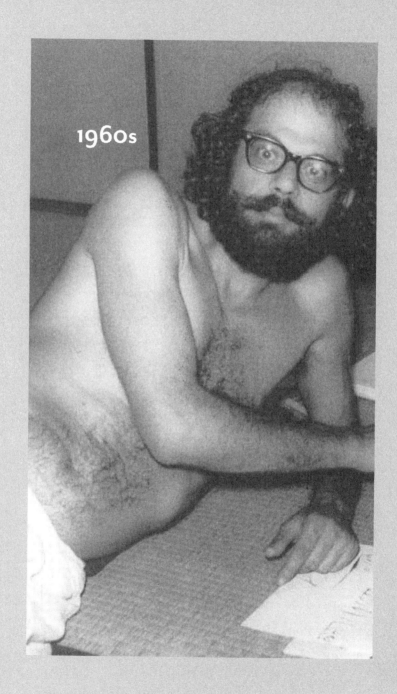

1960s

To Frank O'Hara & John Ashbery
& Kenneth Koch

How real is Bolivia
With its snowy Andes lifting over the modern city
Now that one is in La Paz
Which means the peace in Spanish
Tho the natives speak their native tongue
Especially the women in brown bowler hats
Sitting in the mud with their hands over their noses
Selling black potatoes and blue onions
In the marketplace which covers the hillside
Over which one can see electrical towers
And airplanes landing from Santiago and Lima Caracas
It is strange how real Bolivia is
Its capital cupped in a valley in the Altiplano
Two miles up in the sky
So that I have a headache and continually take aspirin
Which is relatively expensive tho the taxis are 10 cents
And the poverty seems especially created to make me
            seem a Prince
With my beard and black hat and dungarees
Strolling thru the market buying silver flies, spiders &
            butterflies
And green and purple shawls the ladies use
To carry babies and garbage in

While I watch them over rich green pig stews
In the Rembrandtian restaurant filled with waiting
        bearded prophets
Dressed in rags and ancient grey hats over their white
        brows
All the same I feel a little out of place in Bolivia
Which was a beautiful name in my geography book
Lazing alone in my hotel room with two extra empty
        beds
Tho I have seen various unhoused Indian boys
I'd gladly share my solitude with, not knowing their
        names —
And the coca leaf does not really get me high as I
        expected
So that I masturbated 3 times this week
And wrote postcards to all my friends
In NY, Paris, Florence & Kyoto
— I think I'll take a trip to Machu Picchu
Which is a famous Inca ruined city in Peru.

            —*La Paz, Bolivia, April 1960*

Unpublished.

[Poem]

Yesterday I was writing in Heaven or of Heaven
or the day before yesterday, and this morning back
  where
I started from dreaming of man. And
          went to a Turkish Bath
          wrapped my belly in a white towel
          and sat self-conscious in the
                    steam hot room
          staring at my knees

      Then under a shower soaped my balls and ass
Then lay down in the small dark dormitory
with a white cloth over my genitals and
          put my arms behind my head
          and relaxed — a hand crept up my leg
      and a mouth came down on my cock
          and a warm slurp greeted my Mysticism
— but an old German with white hair and steel-rimmed
  glasses
Sneaked in and interrupted the younger Peruvian
and after saluting my knees and belly with kisses
          and further slurps
flopped down to suck, and I thought now after
      4 months OK I'll come —

But the Peruvian
watching hissing in Spanish
heche-te bastante de saliva
make a lot of saliva
The old gentleman lifted his wings and
sat down with his ass over my prick
like a tomb
and began sucking away with his asshole
till I thought I would come
(in an hour) but he quit —

and sucked off the Peruvian
and I lay back with open eyes in the dark
in Lima
and enjoyed my nudity and the creepy sex of the world
waiting for some white-skinned Angel to come
Finish off the job.

— *Lima, Peru, May 26, 1960*

Published as "May 26, 1960" in *Marrahwannah Quarterly*, vol. 3, no. 1 (January 1967), p. 14.

[Poem]

Ayahuasca —
Moonlit nite
entered bamboo roof shelter
lay on ground on robe
— entered the Great Being
     again
— we are all one Great Being
     whose presence is familiar
— To be It, need to be
     also the mosquito
        that bites me
— I am also a mosquito
     on the Great Being

—Peru, June 6, 1960

Published in: *Yage Letters Redux* (City Lights, 2006), p. 101
appendix.

[Poem]

Walt Whitman
    I lost
        Tears again last nite
Screwed out of Heaven
        by a bitter face with eyeglasses
    and a nightstick
        Waving Death over America

Walt Whitman, the fuzz
    is making Fate
    the masses are terrified
        No comrade walks the road
    over mountains overlooks
        the old metropolis from
            under your vast hat —

I was trying to get the Prince to wake up!
    O California
        O soup of anxiety!

— ca. 1960

Published in: *Fuck You: A Magazine of the Arts,* no. 5, vol. 6 (April 1964), p. 5.

Tokyo Tower

On top, the vast city
          100,000,000 people
milky mist, spires of radio
          antennae like Venus —

The Marine Band marching hymn
          without a name on the Jukebox
Fifes and Flutes in Space Drums
          & brass in all bright beauty
way up in the airy window
          crashing around my head

I danced for joy to hear again
          cleansed of all old associations
          the nameless Hymn
          without armies
          in Space.

— Tokyo, Japan, ca. July 1965

Published in: *Ferret,* vol. 2, no. 6 (October 16, 1963), p. 5.

B.C. [Bob Creeley]

I was waiting for Eternals
superimposed on blue sky
and apartment building walls
I was in 15 years before

come back through future doors.
I can't wait forever,
I didn't and came back here
by myself feeling sure

lost in this University
with other males and females
looking in Creeley's live eye,
and we all told similar tales

— San Francisco, October 14, 1963

Unpublished.

War Is Black Magic

War is black magic
Belly flowers to North and South Vietnam
include everybody.
End the human war.
Name hypnosis and fear is the
Enemy — Satan go home!
I accept America and Red China
To the human race.
Madame Nhu and Mao Tse-Tung
Are in the same boat of meat.

—San Francisco, October 30, 1963

Unpublished.

Journals November 22, '63

The black and white glare blink in the inky Air Force
      night
as the Helikopter rose straight up the television frame
carrying President Johnson toward the newsphoto
      White House
past the tail flag of the giant United States of America
      super-jet
settled at rest and lonesome under the klieg light field
swarmed with cops brass photographers mikrophones
      blip McNamara chill
Long nosed Oswald suspect in Dallas of halfmast pro
      Castro assassination

—November 22, 1963

Published in: *Poetry Newsletter,* no. 1 (November 1964), p. 2.

May Day

As the fire burns out tranquility returns
The angry voice at the back of the throat
    softens, and quiet descends
      on the body
The room becomes clear in the
    afternoon light of the stage
The actors talk, growling, the eye
    rests lightly on the invalid
and tenderness sighs from the pit
    of the breast.

Lightness, lightness, as a breeze of
    morphinc, but no fear
in the belly that the police will
    attack
or the rare powder disappear. Ah!
Let's stay where we are in this cafe
    all evening,
No more coffee, I want to sit quiet
    without talking
watching the red haired lady with a cane,
the string of pearls, the slap, the dark
    backs of heads —
Oh shut your filthy mouth! I hate you!

Dad loved me!
Footlights! The heart attack! The gold ring
      screaming in the sunlight.

I tip my head relax'd on my shoulder,
      lean on a table, and gaze thru
      no eyes.

                                                  — *ca. May 1964*

Published in: *Synapse,* no. 3 (January 1965), p. 10.

In a Shaking Hand

Loudspeakers drifting
  clouds of music
Trumpets of prophesy!
Flutes of high-conscious
  Shabda yoga
The giant cranes over
  red buildings —
green railroad bridges
  over the thruway
  to New York
    Temples domes
    & black smoke-
      stacks
in the towers of
  the hilled
    city of brick
Stone iron and glass
  aluminum plastic
George Washington
  High School
    street!
RR arch jumping
  the street valleys
whirling orange curveways

greyhound on
   the dawn line
old apartments on
    green mounts
  rising buttressed in
   the grass road —
Plonk of bass guitars
  New York Mets
   Stadium
The river mysterious
    empty stream
Yankee Stadium's giant
  chest — castellated
  storage warehouse?
Neal at the wheel
  shouting hoarse
  abennied and slept
  & et in the millionaire
   mystic gated
   abode —
Surrounded by river &
  forest, poor dear —
Zawk, Zawk
  Zawk! — the
giant milk
  truck swooping
  up the hill
by the apartment
rise to the skyway overpass

up to the high
elevated
6 lane concrete
Rising thru grey Bronxes
to black railroad
subway flight —
ports
down the curved
bowling alley
so much like S.F. [San Francisco]
The road
grasses & fences

I mean curving balconies
riding — the pink
purple — violined
hearse
over the gunk river
Back under black
Els on their thin
heights —
Oh this endless pro-
liferation of concrete
under the arch bridges
carrying highway above
highway
above their roofs the
buildings baby
faced peeks be low —

windows on the tiny
　　places & things —

Under the fluorescent
　　ceilings below
　　the city —
Higher higher, up the
　　high asphalt balconies
over the calm Harlem
　　　　River
into the artery fluted
　　into the head of the
　　Amsterdam Avenue idiot
　　　at dawn —
old gals in the window
　　spying on the
　　　street —

O hero of Bakersfield!

　　　　　　　— Millbrook to New York City, June 27, 1964

Published in: *Poets at Le Metro*, vol. 15 (July 1964), pp. 4–5.

Little Flower M.M. [Marianne Moore]

I sit three miles from your flat
   glass Manhattan   the bridges grown old
  your breasts   the huge river
      insect steelworks in the Navy Yard

your ears   your mouth pursed   small woman
    in this same night myself   New
      York this Universe
I have a cold you have seventy seven years
     a pain in my chest, I
eat no more meat I smoke much   you
must understand this impulse to confession
     all I can do   a message
may arrive as a soft electric shock of feeling:
Man is no form no mighty molecule no just
     idea alone — all that Thing —
I feel man tender radiance at Heart between
    breast and belly, that physical place
where the Self urges — delicate sensation
    //

I have no children, either
must not moralize. From my breast to yours a
skinny birthday ray.

—New York, ca. October 1964

Published in: Tambimuttu, ed., *Festschrift for Marianne Moore's Seventy Seventh Birthday* (Tambimuttu and Mass, ca. April 1965), p. 100.

Don't Know Who I Am

Don't know who I am
Whether President of Atlantis
  with ruby dancing boys
  longhaired smiling at my baldness
    and teenaged nymphs
  placing small soft hands on my belly fur
Or irresponsible rich prince-garbage man
  of wavy quiet boulevards
    of pacific water
So this minute I accept my
    self
  A big hairy Fish

— *Cambridge, MA, morning, November 12, 1964*

Published in: *Fag Rag*, no. 10 (Fall 1974), cover.

Liverpool Muse

Albion Albion your children dance again
Jerusalem's rock established in the basements of satanic mills

In the *Sink*, stone basement of City
Vibrations of Vox electronic shudder thru brick & flesh,
Children beautifully collared and sleeved, with tapered
        silk dungarees,
each pubescent body thin & handsome shaking his hips,
each darling daughter alone on the concrete snapping
        her fingers —
The longhair guitarist snarls into a silver microphone
    & builds the drum beat to a heavy charge
and screams on the high note — a circle
    of flesh is formed
he screams claps and shudders, a circle of
    flesh dances round,
six boys and two girls, shuffling left
    shuffling right hey hey,
shuffling left shuffling right the Yoruba
    dance step come back to Mersey's Shores —

I stop writing and move my hips —

                              the Circle is
Complete.

—*England, ca. May–June 1965*

Published in: Pete Morgan ed., *C'Mon Everybody* (Corgi Books, 1971), p. 39.

New York to San Fran

And the plane bobs
    back & forth like
    a boat at Kennedy
asphalt Space Station
       glass buildings,
Taking off from Earth, to fly
the day after Stevenson did die
    heart attacked on Grosvenor
      Square's July sunset
        leafy calm.

And I —
    '*Om Om Om*' etc —
repeat my prayers
after devouring the *NY Post*
        in tears —

The radars revolve in their Solitude —
Once more o'er these states
Scanning the cities and fields
    Once more for the Rockies, to look
    down on my own spermy history —

Once more the roar of Life Insurance
        murmuring in the empty plane
                5 hrs 20 min glimpse
The most beautiful Mantra, *'Hari*
        Om Namo Shivaye —'
And the vibration of Shiva
        in my belly merges
        with the groan of machine
                flying into milky sky —

If we should crash the flops of bloody
        Skin won't be singing
                that sweet song —

Once more the green puddles of
        moss in the messy grey bay
once more wingtip lifting to the sun
        & whine of dynamos in the
                stunned ear,
        and shafts of light on the page
                in the airplane cabin —

Once more the cities of cloud
        advancing over New York —
Once more the houses parked like used
        cars in myriad row lots —

I plug in the Jetarama Theater
        sterilized Earphones —

IT'S WAGNER!
THE RIDE OF THE VALKYRIES!
We're above the clouds! The
    Sunlight flashes on a giant
            bay!
    Earth is below! The horns of
    Siegfried sound gigantic in
          my ear —
The banks of silver clouds like mountain
    ranges
I spread my giant green map
    on the air-table —

The Hudson curved below to the
    floor-drop of the World,

Mountain range after mountain range,
    Thunder after thunder,
    Cumulus above cumulus,
        World after world reborn,
    in the ears with the Rhine
        Journey brasses —
          Spacey Sublime
    charges of Aether and Drumbeat
        Ascending & Descending
        the Empty Aeternitas, free —

Click! over upper NY State
    a witty guitar bumps with

pianos & drums — oops!
announcer! oops Peter Sellers
sounds breathing in ye ear
'The Fleshpots! The Muckrakers!'

The little silver cow clouds flow
eastward under the wing,
the horizon's a blue mug, there's
green furze of forest naked &
unpioneered with little
strings of highway & houses
brown pendant —
Lakes with little bungalows —
Once more it's summer and the folks at
ease by their pastoral garages
reading the *Journal American*
Headline screams

100,000 more U S Troops to Vietnam
Adlai Flopped Dead Of Heart Attack On Sidewalk

and a cloverleaf to transport the family
past the Electronic Gasworks —
'Tis the LSD in the balmy upstate
Breeze seeping from Underground
Factory banks —

Switch the channel!
Surf music, oolee!

Plunk of Hawaii, I can feel
the moons, all seven of them
rising over the Mauna Loas
of my Grammar School Decade —
Orange moons, green moons,
blue moons, purple moons,
white moons sinking under wan waves,
Black moons over the lower
                East Side
Red moons over China —

Skipping along one by one,
        bouncing over the cragged horizon
            of Jupiter thru the
                clip clop ethereal violin strings
        and the violas running thru my
            solar plexus,
        they're skipping down the
        Hollywood streets in duck pants
            and 1940s nylon skirts —
It's total Idiocy! a new song
        from the tragic Fiji Island
        love affair, a 30 year old
        teenager weeping into her brassiere,
        her boyfriend's just sailed off
            for Korea and left her
            sobbing with orgasms
                from the Bowery in W W I.

Them plunked guitars and
        descending Melachrino
                — Ugh!
In certain moods it cd / be
        seductive, over the
wingtip it's a Mediterranean
        Blue approaching Cleveland (?)
        hung with puffclouds &
                Hawaiian guitars shining in
                the sunlight —
A children's show! over the
        low Catskills! Speaking in
        a monstrous little voice,
                Pyramus & Thisbe — Up here? —
        The Lion's part, 'you may do
        it extempore for it is nothing but
                        roaring' —
        Distracted from her 'wide body
                in the rain' — I gotta smoke
                some Hashish in the bathroom.

'With impish glee, changes the
        head of Bottom into a donkey' —
and the bottom hills are garden
        green stretched all ways
        with scratch-brown patchy
                valley runnels —
Appears a tray with Old Fashioned!
I'll be drunk before this idiocy's over!

//

Finished the salad and daydreamed of war
and entered the air above checkered farmlands
    to Lake Erie —
I disappeared in a cloud of smoke
        in the plastic lavatory,
    flushing my breath
       down the maelstrom in the toilet —
hours and hours to go o'er America
and beef being served above the white
          carpet-clouds —

A fucking police state! I
    feel at bay, in mid-air!
    'Breaking' the 'Law' — dread
       in the breast guilt in
       the head, as I punched the
          odorous green soap spigot to perfume
        the washbowl & drown
        the sweet Eastern smell
            I carried —

Now I'll make that thornful pilgrimage
on feet of meat & bone across that
        land I see stripped
       & ruled below my
          magic carpeted-cabin.
    Another sip of old fashioned!
    I'll go to jail down there, heart

beating wildly! Not
because love's in my hands,
        buttocks kissed in the Rockies,
    but because this dreamy muzaked
        liquored luxurious air-ride's
        Euphoria's no heaven
If it costs blood-flaps on the smooth
    hairless skin of high cheeked
        Vietnamese teenagers.
Everybody forgets who's body
    suffers the physical pain of Orders
undreamt in these High Air
    Conditioned modern Powers.

Bam! Brahms brasses bang bright bombs
down over Ohio's highways
    I eat meat and a pea
Klemperer changes to *Dance of*
    the Seven Veils, the Head
of John America cut off
    will be presented: Coffee —

And other Channels
    Keep pushing Rock & Roll
    Bottom on Shakespeare, Hallelujah
    Waikiki, Bedtime Story,
    Decline of the West Frug,
    They'll even begin the movie

The Satan Bug after
I finish my cheesecake —

Anything to keep me from looking down
            on that innocent vastitude
Bottomed with Earth speckled
            with townships houses like
            white dots, park centers,

Man has overtaken his universe,
            says the music, and pictures
            of Mars are expected when
                        I set my sneakers on Land —
Beethoven proclaims ethereal Joy!
Strauss is sadder by 2 centuries
            and still the longing strain
            Screams in my ears from
                        middleeurope Concert Halls

I do declare that I am God!
I do declare by my beard & fame
            that I will die!
I do declare war on Satan!
I do declare I am willing to
            take the glory death on
            my hideous stomach
and sing my Prophesy before
            the Nations! —

Hark! ye murderers! Hark
    ye stuffed with vengeance!
Hark ye Angel Recordings! Hark
    ye Joel Sebastian!
May I ask ye Sir Army, whom
    ye hope to Kill?

Hark ye Chicago, the time for
                Earth's Revolution's here!
Hark ye hopeless lovers, thine own
        sweet will be done!
As Huncke came despairing Eastward
        from this blue vast lake,

What misery has been created
    to drown the joyful chant
    of all our souls?

Oh great bend of shore, the men
    on thee too many,
            Chicago flowing with
        red smoke

Pouring out hatred of Communism

It's you angry Hell Hounds
    who have created Stalin and
    his 15,000,000 murdered
        Slavic hysterics —

It's your Capitalism
and your weak suited newsmen
        and your Hearst Bank Mind
that has pushed the Communist
        party to murder
        your own asshole!
It's your bombs over Korea, it
        is your fire in Vietnam, it
        is your shooed diplomat
                across his desk that has lied
                like a Communist bureaucrat
        when the order came to cease the
                penetration of the flesh with
                sharp instruments —

Wagner rides again! Hark
        Ye, Ministers of Power and
        ye Presidents of America
        Ye Premiers of vast China
        and ye Dalai Lamas of
                Tibet —
Hark ye balding soldiers
        reading *Mainliner*
        on the jetplane speeding
        thru the Wagner Dooms
                above these blue
        atomic waters and
        Scratched terrain

above Chicago's tiny
Towers —

At this moment there is a skeletal
man lying on the leafshit cobbles
of Dasawamedh Ghat,
At this moment by our will a
child is beaten in the balls by
a mad communist lieutenant
in an Albanian Phnom-penh —
At this moment Joe Christ Screams
and falls raving on the
neck of a homosexual in Hué —
He bites his neck, he kisses,
he sucks the blood of the corpse —
At this moment a symphony of screams
arises in Uruguay as the riot
is 'quelled' by teeth-bash,
At this moment bombs on Barcelona burst
At this moment the charming children
of Joliet cower in Detention,
planning raids on weak villages
where Me-Kong hath sprouted —

I prophesy thee death, Rock Island
lined with white bungalows —
for thy mean farm's television
only communication to Saigon —
A bank of white cloud advances

as I advance on the Xylophones —
Bongo Rock! Nigeria advances
        with clouds! Earth is
        Hidden in white fleece
        as the drums batter in Mechanic invisibility —
We're all out west, the squares
        of perfect farmland, introduced
        by Thelonious Monk *Off Minor* —
which penetrates these grouped hives
        of suburbia diminutive on the Planet —

That Classical channel always
        resounds thru hemispheres of
            Empty Becoming,
Being filled with drumbeats and total
        orchestra shaking Ascensions
        Crane'd've come to Forever
                If he could —
        Over Indiana, the flutes —
        Over Iowa and Omaha
A technicolor picture begins
        on channel one — Elec
            tronic Bee music.
        The great steel safe door
            crashes shut.
The buzzing sciencefiction
        lights & gauges ascend like
                Brahms didn't —
        A new man is born —

The police answer the telephone —
CIA looks at its wristwatch —

They leave the atomic testing area
                    Goodnight Doctor! —
The glass door   opens automatically,
a wolf runs round the barbed
            wire, it's not state prison,
            it's a scientific laboratory.
Paid for by Hollywood US Govt.
Your own taxes Dearie, it's

            Y O U

Mr Electronics Nightclub
totally disconnected on yon farmhouse
            in mid afternoon amid the
            peaceful buzzing of the cows —
that created this faraway red bongo
            music issuing from tank eyes
            on the screen — your desire
                    by the boathouse.
A yacht on the screen in color
with a gangster spy conversation
            'outspoken on the immorality of war'
        'superb loan operator' . . .
Actually on this screen a confrontation
            a pacifist (who'll turn out
            to be a murderous spiderman?)

'about the most secret chemical
        warfare station on this hemisphere.'

        'Reagan has been murdered and
            Dr. Baxter has vanished' —

So it's not my paranoia
as I ride over these peaceful green
        silent squares of   Anonymous
        Stevenson birthstate —

The movie on this airplane is projecting
        the same angst as my hashish
                bathroom —
So I share in this vast fantasy
which rises like poison gas
from the man-wormed farmlands
        approaching Missouri River —

'There's something beyond the Botulinus —
        Indestructible,'
    our fantasies' guineapig doom —
The germ of Death loosed
            on Earth —
    The sacred drawer opened
        The *Satan Bug*
            Disappeared!
        //

Oh heaven what have we come to
            up here looking down on
                    ourselves,
        man's consciousness is split
                out of his self —
                            'Have they
                            told you
                            just what
                            this new
                            Virus
                            will do?'

'Paranoids . . . they're very
            brilliant the most of them
            — my choice a Messiah'
            as the 'obey or else'
            culprit who stole the
                            Satan Bug.

Shit the movie's attacking
        us Messiahs.

Not in this consciousness can I
        resolve the confusion of Syntax.

        Thin veil above the land,
            the dotted grid of planet smoke —
above the rills' erosions on

brown ploughlands —
(I'm smoking Cancers)

This hashi is depressing,
Or else the mind I'm in,
or else the plane I sit within,
or else the movie croaking in
            the loudspeaker,
or else America itself
        that made the mind movie airplane
                national Paranoia.
'Who is this? Who is this!' on
        the telephone.
                            'We have to get
everyman in the country to find him!'

And westerly the land's become
        Dry brown — and mottled
        with Glacier tracks streaming
            South — Epochs of
Paranoia have come & gone,
The Great White Ice skidded
        its way
                rippling the terrain like
                wind over Summer water,
        the bemedalled soldier lights
            another cigarette —
and now it's flat land and exact
Squares of Arnold's fishing property —

//

Invisible police networks are set
        up in the movie,
    always complaining, always compleynts
    Violins piercing the ears —
        The Glacial skids
         ruining the land for farming
         ½ million years later —

And the clouds've covered the entire
        visible earth;
— that was the Platte I
saw before, streaked with Neal;
now great Rockies streaked
with snow —

Remove the earphones at the
    climax, undivided attention
    to the
        patches of summer snow on
        the razor hills — a
         green valley & its brown road
         settled in between
           black shoulders —
waves of mountains slant
    an inch above the old
        human hummingbird hills —

glacier patches & dust powder
   hollows filled with white cold —
misted over by small vast
      fog —

So I turn back to the
  Satan Bug movie — they're
in a green Ford riding thru desert Utah —
As we pass the sunny Wasatch
  glittering blue south —

Help police! invading a baseball
    diamond
  to find the Doomsday
    Bomb in Los Angeles
  'Power for its own sake!'
Over a grand canyon.
Shake Baby Shake!
  'You've got every reason on
    Earth to be mad.'
And of course the Beatles
  swinging into a Sea of Clouds
    'What this loven man can do,'

Typhoid Mary! We're
  all hypocrites, tell me Why
  The Beatles shouldn't spill the beans
   Secret which might
    Land them in Bedlam,

or Yevtuchenko in Lubyanka
            instead of Spoleto if
                    he spoke without
                            450 corrections.

And if I opened my mouth I'd
be accused of treason in every
            direction, high teacup Jazz,
                    Marxist, Demorep, Castroite, Maoist —
One'd be fallen on and torn to
pieces by Chinese teeth,
American knives, Scouse
            bicycle chains, Vedado
                    cops hairy hands,
Demolished by the Dept. of Social
            Undermining, thrown
            in Ft Leavenworth, sent
            to Siberia, reeducated in
                            Archangel,
            sent to work on a Commune
                    in the fields beneath
                    the Potala.
Meanwhile flying over a red
                    desert, —

Is civilization going to
            Blow up?
                    //

In ten years I've climbed over
    this sunny windowsill John Wieners
Now from Olympian Heights I look
    Down
        on the rough giant earth black
        Streaks of snow on foreign hills
    the vast cloudmass walled
        over the South, above
    the Impenetrable Blue Space
        skied upward
    as Brahms crash swirls
        round my eardrums,
and what should I prophesy,
    Messiah?

The wing tip pierces thru
    mist white Brahms —
I must come back to my body.

No more question but the force
    of wingtip lifting upward
    to reveal the heaven-roof
as music burst
        thru the Stereophonic
        grey tipped earphones
        Vast as the visible
        Universe —
        //

Our desires pounding on,
our desire mounting, past Mars,
our hearts beating a million years,
Otto Klemperer enraged on
                the podium,
Salomé dancing again in
        the airplane cabin,

Demands of the Beethovenian fist
                in the Lightningstorm!

I am that I am,
        renewed week after week,
    planeride after planeride,
                Despair after streetcorner
                        headache despair.
Joyfully flying to death,
        till the atom cellular
                consciousness invades
        with its cancerous stabs and
            flashes of electric chair.
All so solid it can't even be a
                dream
Tho the phantom orgasm
        of paraplegics proves
you can come in pure
        Consciousness
    & spurt your semen all over

a dreamwall bordello
          painted blue in Lima
while the groin's dead
     limp & wrinkled under
     the transparent cellophane
          sheets of Experiment.

It's too sad! It's too happy!
It's here, unfolding like
     a giant rose,
It changes slow as eternity
     shifts, it flies in triumph
     thru the western clouds,
it approaches its old
     memory city to find
     its loves grown old & sane
     and its own body middleaged
It flies toward old wrinkled faces,
It's inexplicable, it rises
     Triumphant above the Very
          Earth and Screams
          in Delight
                    over
          the cumulus clouds.
Fasten your seatbelts in
          the Mist!
     The violins are ascending in
          every direction!
               //

'We have climbed to 35,000 feet!'
The desert flows like a river
   thru the mountain passes,
     wrinkled like our own faces
       above the smooth sand.

Nevada's rough belly
   breathless below!

I'll get drunk & give no shit,
   & not be a Messiah.
      and have long talks goofing
      with Wieners in Belvedere
        by a stinky pond,
          drinking Dorian Gray martinis.
And 'twixt earnest & joke
     Enjoyed the Ladeye, John.
We're stuck in our
       Selves.
And who else to be stuck in?
     A courteous Astronaut come
       down from the Horizon
   to gaze in our eyes with patience,
   take our hand, and lift it
   trembling, to his khaki breast —

Half the visible universe
excluded from this fantasy
but who's counting?

Mama? God? Dear widowered
                  Olson? Creeley
stumbling over his pecker?
Me, murmuring, what a beautiful
            big pecker you got to a
            pimply 16 year old boy
                  with his pants down on
                  my pallet,
      who talked all night about his
            intellectual disorders
      till my belly softened & I kissed
            him on his shirt?

Beethovenian Climaxes Impossible?
Wagnerian Valkyric rides
            Immaterial?
Salomé dances too Incredible?
What're we groveling in but the
            most magnificent Aluminum Heaven?
            complete with transcontinental
                  cloudcities —
      Complete with million horsepower
            Jetroar astounding to any
                  pre war Daedalus —

Clouds racing eastward, the
      plane lowering slowly thru
            the veils, over the

flat Sacramento valley,
                    Down

into the inhabited shores,
the myriad minute boxes stacked
        in rows, curved in clusters
        planted like vast letters in
                the giant flats
above the empty silent Space-
        hangar in South Peninsula —
Over the Bay, pointing toward
                Golden Gate & Tamalpais
Home,
        to the weak sad destiny
        of aging companion selves
trembling above the red broadcasting
                        towers,
Down to the brown rippled
        water, past yacht basin parks
past outdoor movies empty
        sunlight glaring off the
                white billboards,

OM, Down to the
ground roar tremble
        along the white line
        Jetbrakes roaring,
                Brahms screaming
        Symphony concluding

as we taxi slowly
        down the runway
to the metalvoiced
            Terminal,
                United.

—*Finit 7:30 p.m., July 15, 1965*

Published in: *City Lights Journal,* no. 3 ([January 1] 1966), pp. 108–28.

Entering Kansas City High

Entering Kansas City high
  thin trees lining the highway wire balcony
    over the Gulf, lit with orange flares
    in the smoke in front of the green signs
      where all-night factories pin-point grey-
   clouded space illumined
  blue bright craned robot lamps.

Street after street each valley dark at midnight
  rooms and attics lit, hills banded with caterpillars
    of street illumination
  high-tension wires across the railroad track mid-
    city
      Kansas and Missouri meeting
        7th Street North Business District fine
        black mist
      winking antenna
        lights Sensitive City, ooh!
 Crost the wheeled bridges
   by wheat elevators' rounded parade
   red U.S. Mail box blue-legged on the
     sidewalk
      a huge truck stopped at a red light
   roar of jet harshness on the sky ear

For Sale an old brown cabin
            along the road by Smitty's Bait Minnows
                Eat:
                    Air Reduction, Ohio Chemical
                        another viaduct above lone railroad
                            track assemblage of switch and
                                switch-light shack,
                                    underneath river highway
                                lights
                                        reflected doubled
        along the curved level silver-black water,
          the fear
                    of the police state under the bridge,
        tail lights speeding up the alley
                under the super highway overpass
                    concrete-vaulted
        an instant later, the iron-ringed auto bridge   and
                    sentinel stacks lit again with their feeding
                        ladders aluminum'd

    Up the shining asphalt, lit-blue
            outskirts' roads and trailers parked camping
                row on row under the hill.
        Rainbow Boulevard at night   Kansas U Medical
            Center
                    Greek column'd, mid-American brick
                        Jewel
                            Restaurant, with a little church with a
                                cross held

                    thinly above its door,
        and the State Drive-in Bank, Safeway
                empty-lit   Brain-blood volume increased
        stopped in a side street   Club 423 red signs.

                            —*Midnite, February 12, 1966*

Published in: *Great Society,* no. 1 (1966), p. 10.

Cleveland Airport

Cafeteria's metallic counter, iced tea & a blue check,
a yellow haired baby long tressed kissing father's shaven
   cheek,
        fluorescent ceiling re-mirrored thru plate glass
            over parkinglot darkness,

Melancholy to sit here middle-aged
   with worn sleeve & hairy hand
      exposed, alone.

—June 8, 1966

Published in: Allen Ginsberg, *Scrap Leaves* (Poet's Press, 1968),
p. 7.

Busted

How many people have been busted?
How many people, their doors broken down,
        dragged weeping in their nightgowns
                to the station?
How many boys been slapped around
        by midnight cops downtown in
                the colored section?
How many musicians pushed out of jobs?
How many students kicked out of school?
How many businessmen hiding paranoiac behind their
        doors afraid of disgrace
            by narco bulls
                hiding behind guns and badges
    with their ignorance and misinformation?
How many cats shaken down beaten up &
        asked for payoffs by Treasury fuzz?
How many pounds of pot seized & sold on black market
                by cops?
How many scholars and doctors pressured,
        warned, blackmailed, prosecuted?
How many newspapers radio stations bombarded with
        dopefiend T-man propaganda?

What divine congressional investigation will ever undo
all these decades of calumny, injustice,
brainwash, jail?

— 1966

Published in: *High Times,* no. 225 (May 1994), p. 36.

Nashville April 8

Crescent faces row-tiered hanging
   balconied face the great red
Striped flag podium microphonic reverberation
      from one body outward
breathed painfully from rich suited abdomen
— mouth opening circle of white teeth — bells
    clanging
    Taillights along the Nashville city edge —
      In the leather car, acrid perfume
      sucked in the lung,
   Majesty of Speech and Chant, on the lawn
      Under the streetlight
dry grass crowded with sweating college shirted blond
    & forehead-starred' Semite singing —
In the far cities riot under the Spring
moonless midnite Black Power.

—April 8, 1967

Published in: *Spectrum*, vol. 5, no. 3 (Spring 1967), pp. 24–25.

After Wales Visitacione July 29 1967

The Great Secret is no secret
    Senses fit their rosy winds —
Visible is visible, rain mist
    curtains wave thru the bearded vale —
Foxgloves erect green buds, mauve
    bells droop trembling doubled down
    the stem, spiked antennae —
Daisies push their inch of yellow air,
No imperfection on the budded mountain,
valley vegetables tremble, horses dance
      in the warm rain
white sheep speckle the mountainside & move eating
      green atoms shimmer
    in grassy mandalas
Blue atoms shimmer in the sky, grey atoms wet the
Wind's Kabbalah
A solid mass of Heaven, mist-infused, ebbs thru the
    Vale, a wavelet of Immensity lapping gigantic
    thru Llanthony Valley
motion at the bottom of the sky,
earth rolls the days, sun hangs
    the planet on its lightbeams
Mists drawn from the ocean & driven like lambs thru
    the

meadows of Wye to these mounts, to the
                    edges of London —
pheasants croak flapping up from Fern steep
    meadow —
Heaven shifting its cloudy floor on the
    million feet of daisies
Each flower Buddha-eye, buds mirroring eyeball
    manufactured many
Sat on a rock crosslegged in dusk rains
slit eyed, breath steady, mind moveless,
My own breath
        trembles the white daisies by the roadside,
The breath of Heaven and my own breath
symmetric,
        central emptiness manifests body
        giant valley veined with tree-lined
canals manufactured over centuries,
sprouty bushes fringing houscholds walls, hill
breast nippled with hawthorn,
belly meadows haired with fern —
Same breath that waved in the valley
    drawn into my belly, slowly breathed
— Sounds of Aleph & Aum
        thru forests of gristle, my skull
& Lord Hereford's Knob an equal windy place —
                to my navel the
    same breath as breathes thru Capel-y-ffin,
        All Albion is one!
Stokely Carmichael flying on the same wind to Cuba

angry at the windy thistle's silly thorns?
News of the World ploughs in abstract fields
to harvest money not physical potatoes in silence,
& the physical sciences and in ecology, that is
    the wisdom of earthly relationships,
                mouths and eyes interknit
    hoof, wing & leaf
bearing the giant body forward 10 centuries in
         Llanthony,
orchards of mind language manifest human —
cows and sheep pass by twos to death
    horses born for cancer of the snout —
I lay on a hill and entered Wales in Visitacione nameless
      bard on her hill thru Blake's eye,
         Wordsworth's particular thistle,
Stare close, no imperfection in the grass, symmetric
         Maya
    covering moist ground, smell of brown Vagina,
         harmless.
The whole mass of Heaven balanced on a grassblade,
          Gigantic sun at the end of heaven
    & the lightest rose at the cottage door
    weighed equal, on the exquisite scales
              trembling everywhere
    in balance the death of a brown grassblade, the
    birth of a soft mushroom
Sheep look up revolving their jaws with empty eyes,
             pacific gods
    little gods that look at me curious & keep distant

from human fame.
Creatures revolving thru births and deaths, unharmed
    horses in a tiny gigantic vale in Wales.
I am Bard to my own nature nameless as the very Vast I
    look at.
Lay down on the warm hillside & groaned release from
    my body
    sighed thru my breast a great Ooh!
    Knelt before the thorn,
a mammal aware in the warm grass that smelled of my
    sperm,
    mixing my beard with the wet hair
    of the mountainside, tasting the violet
hair of the thistle, sweetness.
                    Lifted my head and groaned.
Water from the sky came making noise, as
    I babble to vastness
    Earth and sky met and made noise between them
Death's black angel lifted
white fleshed day in his arm for a joyous kiss — in
the afternoon rain.

                    —Wales and London, July 29–August 2, 1967

Published in: *La Huerta*, vol. 1, no. 3 (1973), pp. 57–60.

Mabillon Noctambules

Baudelaire's Noctambules
Old Navy, Lipp, street cafes
   Crowded chattering
autos exploding on cobblestone
grey St. Germain stone's stillness
      Mabillon broods
   with a beard oxygen shadow,
Lovers walk hand in hand with
         empty eyes
Beautiful youths grow pimples sleeping
   on the Seine with the police
   under Notre Dame's silent
      grey lacework —
Sad, as bored Apollinaire gave up
   the ghost on Pont Mirabeau
Sad, as Tzara sat at Deux Magots
   collating spit-soiled letters
        from Artaud
Sad, as Michaux walks solitary
   down Rue Segur to the Seine
      brooding loveless —
Sad, as the cafes close for
   the summer,
Sad, as a decade ago I shopped

in Rue de Seine for mussels
with Orlovsky weeping in bed
Gregory upstairs in fury
    scribbling American
Burroughs enchambered considering
        Silent blues —
Sad, as no poets emerged from
    the streets, gaiety eyes
        & eyebrows sharp with
                new Francs
    not old eternity, not old
        Sadness of Meat realizing
        Frenchness a moment
enthusiastic as the virgin belly of Jean-Arthur
    arriving in Paris bedbugged
        Screaming in melodious slang —
Merde! Le Con! Salaud! shriek
    the bourgeois sharpies with
        shaved short hair at the zinc bar,
    bored with their jamais & red girls
No music, no magic Vulnerables
    in manly wristwatches —
No beautiful faces on these
    ancient streets yet —
I've been faithful w/ my beard
                10 years,
& now arrive in silken gold-crost robe
hair perfumed & long, hero of
    my own universe

& sit in the White Queen at 2 A.M.
recalling the ghosts of Paris, of the
    50s as Hemingway
in Montana lamented a thought for a night
    of the Great Lesbians
       shining in 1924 surrounding Cloiserie
    de Lilas —
Bill Myself Peter & Gregory the
    angels of pain a decade
      incognito
The barman's bald, I'm bald,
    & Gregory's broke in New York —
More ghosts as sad as ourselves will
    pass St. Sulpice or gaze
over the chimneyed roofs & mansards
    curved along the Seine
Wondering what magic of Paris
    was promised, what charm
that now's the fat barman spilling
    blue-labeled lemonade
over the stainless steel drain.

—Paris, 2:20 a.m., August 25, 1967

Published in: *Big Sky*, no. 10 (1976), pp. 130–131.

Genocide

Dreamed, that I met Leroi
his American speech slightly thickened &
slurred from learning Yoruba
& thinking in Afric syntax —
   We lay together, our
legs wrapped & twined round
each other's bodies, soft cheeks
together, I had difficulty making
out his words, and though he
was not aloof and I thought
he spoke against my Jews,
flashed thru my mind to
tell him this fault, I
listened instead, and sad
said "What will happen
to me Leroi? I may
perish for all this War
in America" — He lay his
head next to mine & held
me close, dawning on me
his tragic fear & sympathy
all along despite what
the newspapers said — But
dont remember his dream

words as murmured, far away,
& his body brown & warm as
we pressed our breasts together,
I felt his hard on at first,
which went away as we
clung closer. He wanted
to protect me in the War
storm, but was unable
for the great force that was
upon us, of strangeness and
alien white mind in America,
rising from Iowa, Kansas,
Nebraska, Wisconsin, Brooklyn.

—Cedar Falls, Iowa, February 23, 1968

Published in: Diane di Prima, ed., *War Poems.* (The Poets Press, 1968), pp. 37–38.

No Money, No War

Government Anarchy prolongs illegal
planet war over decades in Viet-nam. Federal
Anarchy plunges U.S. cities into violent chaos.

Conscientious objection to war tax payment
subsidizing mass murder abroad and
consequent ecological disaster at home will
save lives & labor and is the gentlest
way of political revolution in America.

If money talks, several hundred
thousand citizens refusing tax payments
to our War Government will short-
circuit the nerve system of our
electronic bureaucracy.

—December 16, 1969

Published in: *Tax Talk* (ca. December 29, 1969), p. 4.

1970s

May King's Prophecy

Spring green buddings, white-blossoming trees, Mayday
      picnic
O Maypole Kings Krishnaic Springtime O holy Yale
Panther Pacifist Conscious populace awake alert
      sensitive tender
children's bodies — and a ring of quiet Armies around
      town —
planet students cooking brown rice for scared
      multitudes —
Oh souls all Springtime prays your bodies
quietly pass mantric peace Fest grass freedom thru our
      nation
thru your holy voices' prayers
your bodies here so tender & so wounded with Fear —
Metal gas fear, the same fear whales tremble war
      consciousness
Smog city — Riot court paranoia — Judges, tremble!
      Armies weep your fear —
O President guard thy sanity
Attorneys General & Courts obey the Law
and end your violent War Assemblage
O Legislatures pass your Creeds of order
& end by proper Law illegal war!

Now man sits Acme Conscious over his gas machine
     covered Planet —
Springtime's on, for all your sacred & satanic magic!
Ponds gleam clouded heaven — Black voices chant thru
     car radio
Oh who has heard the scream of death in jail?
Who has heard the quiet Maytime Om beneath wheel-
     whine and drumbeat
In railyards on wire tower'd outroads from New Haven?

                              —*New Haven, CT, May 1, 1970*

Published in: *Strike Newspaper* (May 2, 1970), p. 3.

For the Soul of the Planet Is Wakening

For the soul of the planet is
Wakening, the time of dissolution
of material forms is here, our
generation's trapped in Imperial
Satanic cities & nations, & only
the prophetic priestly consciousness
of the bard — Blake, Whitman
or our own new selves — can
steady our gaze into the
fiery eyes of the tygers of the
Wrath to come

—before September 21, 1970

Published as a broadside: *For the Soul of the Planet Is Wakening*
(Desert Review Press, 1970).

Six Senses

Hiss, gaslamp —
     Night wind shakes leaves.

*

Hemp smoke in wood hall,
Kerosene leaked at lampbase
                    knocked off desk.

*

Yellow light on knotted wall,
     Aladdin chimney, brass
     wick cutter, pencil bottle
          plastic passport, staple shine.

*

Who am I? Saliva,
     vegetable soup,
                    empty mouth?

*

Hot roach, breath smoke
    suck in, hold, exhale —
        light as ashes.

*

Eye lids heavy, dreamed yesterday dawn
    kissing the two eyed horse.

                    —*Xmas Meditation on Milarepa, 1970*

Published in: *Coyote's Journal*, no. 9 (1971), back cover. In addition
the fourth and fifth parts have been collected in Ginsberg's
Collected Poems, but not the other four parts.

[Poem]

Frank O'Hara darkly
hearing *Così Fan Tutte*
scratches his nose.

—ca. 1970

Published in: *Clothesline,* no. 2 (1970), p. 36.

[Poem]

Hum! Hum! Hum!
    Gregory Corso's genius despised,
Muses bored,
    Mediocrity is prized —
Bullshit the award.
    Hum! Hum! Hum!

—ca. early 1971

Published in: *Washington Post* (March 3, 1971), p. C1.

[Poem]

The world's an illusion
Everybody dies the day after they graduate High School

—August 30, 1971

Published in: *Embers* (Wayne Valley Senior High School, 1972),
p. 134.

Reef Mantra

. . . Blue Starfish
    Violet minnow,
        Sea cucumber
           Coral tide . . .

—Fiji, March 3, 1972

Published in: Allen Ginsberg, *First Blues* (Full Court Press, 1975), p. 35.

Postcard To D

Chugging along in an old open bus
    past the green sugarfields
        down a dusty dirt road
            overlooking the ocean in Fiji
thinking of your big MacDougal street house
    & the old orange peels
        in your mail-garbage load
           smoggy windows you clean with a
        squeegee —

                —Fiji, March 3, 1972

Published in: Allen Ginsberg, *First Blues* (Full Court Press, 1975), p. 34.

Inscribed In George Whitman's
Guest Register

Cold January ends snowing on sidewalks,
Millions of kids cry & sing in Lowell,
Massachusetts is full of bearded pubescent saints,
Notre Dame's lit up white as Whitman's beard,
I got a $1 wool suit from Salvation Army and a tie
flowered from 1967 and a new round watch
& no beard, & Gregory a leopard spotted coat
on his back returned your *Pomes Pennyeach* —
talking of Jonathan Robbins the punk Jersey Rimbaud,
& Brion's operation, & who's been in & out the
        bookshop
— This morning acid wakefulness overlooking the
        Seine
Gregory claimed death's democracy while the river
        streets
floated in Eternity eyeballed from the balcony, solid
evanescent apartments under a grey familiar sky —
Back and forth to Paris, utopian socialists' beards grow
        longer
and whiter — someday the whole city'll be white as
        Notre

Dame's snow-illumined facade, George's goatee, this
page

—Shakespeare & Co. Bookshop, Paris, ca. 10 a.m.,
January 31, 1976

Unpublished.

On Farm

Noisy beets boiling in the pressure cooker
Gas mantle mirrored white gold in the window
Answering letters, September first midnight

—Cherry Valley, NY, September 1, 1973

Published in: *Bombay Gin,* no. 7 (Summer/Fall [1980] 1979), p. 82.

Wyoming

A mountain outside
a room inside
a skull above

Snow on the mountain
flowers in the room
thoughts in the skull.

—Teton Village, WY, November 1973

Published in: *Poetry Project Newsletter,* no. 11 (January 1, 1974), p. 6.

Exorcism

You're going to grow old, white haired withered gasping
stretched on sick-room bed helpless conscious oxygen
tent paralyzed
Several days secure immobile protected in coma
Fortunate karma, family billions, born power wealth
nurses richest doctors & medicines the world
unguents, attendants, gases, needles, morphines private
suites —
Then suddenly realize no help — coma spreading thru
brain nerves
— your power Powerless, your money sand, dreamtime,
illusion
Lonely as an arthritic-handed charwoman washing the
floor in your skyscraper —
You stare at the ceiling and disappear, board rooms and
Arabian derricks vanish with your extinction
Remember pain suffering you caused others Power
Head!
Stop & Frisk laws on your deathbed conscience! No-
Knock you introduced the Nation 1963
Anyone's head bashed to the door — police in his own
home no warning —
fragile in hospital sheets remember your tough-
mouthed Violence Governor

Built insubstantial buildings highways drained liquid
        chemicals
from earth to spread over unsuspecting mortals
        poisoning their air
Crazy cars roam the landscape lonesome scared of your
        police — You worshipped petroleum bank's
        money monopoly with your brothers —
Your anger ordered massacre the guards and prisoners
        Attica Prison yard
How you hid in your Albany mansion reading papers on
        your lap
willing Mass Murder in Jail while junkies screamed Stop
        their Torture
How you screamed back a year later in front of Labor
        Unions to send junkies to death!
Yea you money addict power fixer petroleum pusher
grow whitehaired sickened frail someday, body pained,
        gasping for morphine
on deathbed remember Ego's actions & hatreds
Strangle to death as I will Governor, no guards protect
        you
Die blind wondering where the President went —
Reborn a red necked cursing gas station attendant on
        thruways paved in Hell
Because you pounded the table mandatory death
        penalty for junkies 1973

You energy-junkie Nelson Aldrich Rockefeller be reborn
in your own image.

—January 28, 1974

Published in: *Seven Days* (October 5, 1974), p. 7.

Eyes Full Of Pitchpine Smoke
(by Allen Ginsberg and Gary Snyder)

Eyes full of pitchpine smoke
    Ears full of frogs
How can I keep my books?

          Pitchpine smoke
        drives mosquitoes crazy
    they all go over to the Greensfelders

   Bookkeeping in the moonlight
   — frogs count
       my checks.

—Kitkitdizzie, CA, June 16, 1974

Published in: *End,* no. 9 (1975), p. 24, and the third section
"Bookkeeping in the moonlight…" is in Ginsberg's *Collected Poems*
as one of "Sad Dust Glories."

Freedom of Speech

Freedom of speech
Oh yeah, scared of the cops
freedom of speech
I'm an average citizen
scared of the cops
freedom of speech
I'm an average citizen
scared of the cops

That's my attitude
That's my attitude too
That's my attitude
That's my attitude too
That's my attitude
That's my attitude too

—Boulder, CO, ca. June 1975

Unpublished.

Green Notebook

Nothing lonelier
than on a Greyhound
crossing Donner Pass
Superhighway 80
thru Truckee to Reno
age 20,
rolling on concrete
past pines icy
Castle Peak.

—ca. 1975

Published in: Allen Ginsberg, *Sad Dust Glories* (Workingmans Press, September 18, 1975), p. 3.

Imagination
(by Gregory Corso and Allen Ginsberg)

Magnifying &
transmitting
unworded
eyebrain
on command

manikins
from the compartment
wallpaper
the cockpit
with star-come

Megagalactic
Broadways
delight
Buddha-junkies
Muhammad-Ali-fight

Wipe
the muleteer
shitface
off the Zoroastrian-mount
Fly
//

unwing'd-thought
mechanics
into the see-mind
Fish
with eyes like mine

for aery sharks
no DNA
remembers

Vivid
pilots
cosmosian-skinned
land

—Paris, January 30, 1976

Published in: *Beatitude*, no. 29 ([August] 1979), p. 50.

[Poem]

Spring night four a.m.
Garbage lurks by the glass windows
Two guys light a match
Smoke rolls over Eighth Street where
Spade queens walk lipsticked looking for a taxi
Spoon out their handkerchiefs
Coughing against the black dust rising up
Out of Imiri Baraka's latest volume of poems

The *Whole Earth Catalogue* up in flames
The water pumps methods for making home-made
       yogurt
The crackling red fires running over the San Francisco
       Communal catalogue
Herbert Marcuse exploding in flames
Howl, fiery volume after volume
Over the precipice

Fire spreads through the Skira catalogues
The Rembrandt canvas girl
Brown holes appear in priceless Van Goghs, Roman
       statuaries
Smoke covered smudged Venus de Milo
    //

Up on the front in embers Andy Warhol's *Philosophy From
A To B*
Tennessee Williams autobiographical life in ashes
William Carlos Williams' poetry follows him
To a white dusty grave
Shakespeare himself leaves not a rack behind

— *New York City, ca. May 6, 1976*

Published in: *Villager,* vol. 44, no. 20 (May 13, 1976), p. 2.

Louis' First Night In Grave

Surrounded by transmission wires
and tombstones with old names
the sound of trains and auto tires
protested modern claims —

Weeping a little, earth thrown down
on your coffin lid
oblivion you called your town
Newark wherein you hid

Came out to see your fresh dug grave
red earth, as rounded Rose
the family gather'd, what could save
your memory, what we chose.

I knew the earth that covered you
was your own choice of bed
that year had water often true
of the highway we drove that led

To a small graveyard outside Newark
where remnants gather'd round
families that remember'd the odd quirk
That made you sing in sound

//

Aunts & uncles of old times
Silent movie cousins
Grandfathers whose faces mime
grandchildren by the dozens.

Brothers tearless in the mist
Sisters silent in fog
Nephews whose dead lips were kissed
gold haired children in smog

Poets of the days of youth
Passed, and were forgotten
Brothers in law dead in the booth
of Belmar's wharves gone rotten

Sisters uncles cousins passed
Friends from olden days
Drawers of the laundry cart,
Drugstore brothers ways —

Now I am fifty, olden days
echo like a chord
familiar from old phonographs
or photographs of yore —

Tears, tears and weeping thoughts
Sighs sighs & tears

All the world is swept away
as your coffin steers

Its way down underneath the earth,
down below life and breath
Form is emptiness and birth
Shows my Father's death

It's midnite on your burial day
I sit at your old desk
rhymes running thru my head that lay
a music on your breast —

Legs once strong were withered, now
can't support the player
Silent still and settling underground
layer under layer etc.

To capture all that golden look
Naomi gave to you
& you gave to your own true love
would be something olden new

Clear, sight and yellow sun
air, trees and moon
Shine still over Paterson
as when you were young
//

Trollying to highschool class
Thru the farmer's fields
Newark to Paterson you'd pass
Industry's new wheels

Now silence sits and buzzes in
The house you lived in long
a silent candle in the living room
burns all this one night long

Edith sleeps and sighs and dreams
I sit up late at night
Heavy hearted that my youth
and yours, are gone from sight

Candle that with yellow flame
keeps the watch for me
while you spend your first night at home
in new eternity

—ca. July 9, 1976

Unpublished.

Kidneystone Opium Traum
(for Michael Brownstein)

Its always acting like that beginning
you get in your car & drive in the opposite direction
lock bumpers with a truck going backward
Get out & taxi to the railroad station
Its bombed out & empty in Munich or its Albany
Suspicious of the train schedule suspicious of hot dogs
Suspicious of this suspicious, of that, you take a plane
to Hawaii and act suspicious at the baggage check-in
You delay the flight an hour arguing with the pilot
Suspicious the plane will take you by mistake to Buenos
   Aires
You want to go to Hong Kong but don't know the way
By foot impossible, by boat too long, by super jet
suspiciously easy. Burroughs always wanted a slow boat
to China but you didn't, you're suspicious of all forms of
   transportation —
Cash in your ticket let's go home, let's stay where we
   are —
I'm suspicious of any move you'll make

      —Boulder, CO, ca. August 3, 1977

Published in: *Portage* (1978), p. 36.

Homage to Paris At The Bottom Of The Barrel

(for Philip Lamantia)

Take your god Shuddering morsel
Take delicious Lipstick
God white pussycat
Tiger moon dropped on the roof
Your god Snowflake
Gold ears Celluloid eyelids
Plaster Paris Poet bust
Take your god unreasonable Mamma
Pythagorean spaghetti
Your god oregano Henna
Hermetic multiplication of red Semen
Like solid matter kidneystones
Banana republic grammarschool silkstocking muscles
Your god Spittle-heart God atombomb
Crashed thru time like an umbrella
Descending from the Chrysler Building
O Chorusgirl God
Chant Radio City Music Hall forever
Hula hula purple gardens green sunsets
Volcanic ash sliding off your skull

With noise like a wet apple core falling into the
  wastepaper basket.

—ca. 1977

Published in: David Applefield, et al., *Fire Readings* (Frank Books,
1991), p. 133.

[Poem]

Bebbe put me on your lap
Belly up and Jack me off
Harder Harder suck me off
Bebe I'm old I'm old
I can't come I want you to see me
straining naked Help me Help me
come Please I can't you make me
This is me This is me ah this is me —
I want you to suck my thick cock
yes this is me Please this is me

—March 6, 1978 1:30 a.m.

Published in: *United Artists,* no. 12 (January 1981), p. 101.

Verses Included In *Howl* Reading
Boston City Hall

. . . when the blonde & naked angel came to pierce
      them with a sword
who were busted for eye-contact in the Boston Public
      Library men's room
when a handsome youthful policeman flashed his Irish
      loins & winning smile over urinal, & then
      exhibited his badge
who were arrested for teenage porn ring headlines in
      Boston Globe when the octogenarian bachelor
      D.A. got hysterical screaming through his iron
      mask at election time
lusting lusting lusting for votes, for heterosexual
      ballotboxes' votes,
who arrested bus driving fairies & put them in an iron
      cage, & yelled at little homeless boys
& made them sing and dance in tears to please the
      plainclothes courts
& fink on lonesome middleaged bearded lovers
      kneeling to worship kid Dionysus in Revere

Lord of orgies, ecstasies, poolhalls & pinball machines
set up by Syndicate near the old amusement
park freakshow fronting Atlantic Ocean . . .

—Boston, April 1978

Published in: *Fag Rag,* no. 23/24 (Fall 1978), p. 1.

All the Things I've Got to Do

Things I gotta do
I remembered
when I sat down to meditate
after weeks wandering streets of iron thoughts
I have to go back to the universe
Buddha imagination
Practice path, four foundations and castle of thousand
        days mental breath exercise
But on this desk Friday and Saturday *New York Times*
its Monday noon's lost news
Seven Days the pacifist radicals' temporary magazine
St. Marks Church Poetry Newsletter, the *Society of Useful*
        Manufacturers Newsletter
and poems from Paterson's souls born after the acid
        wars
Does Murray Kempton's book *Briar Patch* really prove
        that the FBI's Gene Roberts started the New
        York chapter of the Black Panthers?
This Gene Roberts witnessed Malcolm X's assassination
        on stage up in Harlem as his bodyguard
a government agent
Scott Nearing approved Stalin
but his *Making Of A Radical,* enlightened my momma's
        history

hereby also Irving Rosenthal's letter from anonymity
the True Levelers tilling common land in Cobham,
           England April 1, 1649
"Digge up, manure and sowe corn upon George Hill in
           Surrey"
Free, Irving Rosenthal proclaims
As I look out my $300 a month apartment window in
           New York at TV antennae under gray sky on
           the Lower East Side
I can't write this poem I got too much to do
Of Time and The River and *The Web In The Rock* on my desk
old second hand books I found
got to read it before I die
The *Yipster Times*, old police state news,
David Erdman's *Symmetries of the Song of Los*
a paper on my bookshelf a year
and my Musiphonic radio which once stood on my
           father's desk
Mahler's symphonies flying through the air
my dirty red bandana needs washing, windows too
six foot bookshelf of unread Buddhist classics
Lotus Sutra and haikus, telephone ringing
young scholar ear waiting my attention
desk with 365 unanswered letters
undigested news clips to file under CIA FBI Cosa Nostra
           dope surveillance lies & truths in my cabinet
           file drawers
ten years journals now typed

I haven't edited the misspellings and blanks the typist
    left
anti-nuclear protest decade now
consider a factory loft on Mill Street, Paterson
can I go home again?
A farm to till and pay nut trees for next generation
Thin out my bedroom library
Keep Plato, Prajnaparamita, David Cope and Gampopa
Visit my stepmother Mother's Day
A brother to cheer
Nephews to make money for and rescue from the
            mental bomb
best friend to call, his day off Monday
A poetry secretary to instruct correspondence
a poem on junk mail to recall
I'll get up now
breakfast and talk to George Balmer before I xerox my
            Blake music sheets
edit Shambhala's *Talking Poets* and read up my file on
            nuclear poison.

                                        —*early May 1978*

Unpublished.

No Way Back to the Past

On the Ferris Wheel rising to the full moon
by the canal, looking down on Ocean Grove
over a red-bulb-rooft green-lit carousel, silver Chariot of
        Muse with her Lyre, revolving all too fast
through years from 1937 with cousin Claire in Asbury
        Park
wandering Sunday morning from Belmar with a few
        pennies dimes for tickets in Playland —
the wire-mesh railed cage swinging under a canvas-
        flowered awning toward the full moon forty
        years later,
a bent hunchback at the gate pulling his iron-rod
        handle to bring the iron-spoked circle hung
        with pleasure cars to rest.
Whacky shack's painted toy-wizard witch-monster
        window
Machinery's laughing screaming lifting wooden eyelids
at fair skinned blond boys rubber-bumping electric cars
        along a sheet-tin floor,
with trolleypole antennae sliding and sparking across
        the silvery ceiling.
I used to ride the skooter with my cousins Clare and Joel
        Gaidemack or brother Gene,
cars shocking lightly on the happy floor, wheeling the

           toy Dodgem in a circle
turning round the curve, I looked up in the mirror
and saw a bald white bearded man in a white shirt
           staring in my eyes —
and entered in the giant wood barrel-form slippery
           rolling underfoot reflecting mirrored through
           its other end *Time Tunnel,*

Time in the car with stepmother Edith at the wheel
           returning from the shore, the panic of Eternal
           space unchanging
through which our phantom bodies pass now highway
           grandeur'd under blue sky.
And poor little Clarie's gone, a ghost in my mind —
walking the big sandy beach, jumping granite boulders
           sharp edged on the jetty with
all us who played Jungle Camp in the Belmar weed-
           grown empty lot's leafy bower
before going to Asbury, the Mayfair Theater Sunday see
           Paul Muni's movie *Dr. Pasteur.*
One family house, sat on the porch at night and beat
           away the mosquitoes
near the tiny Playland where Eugene worked, by a 20
           foot Ferris wheel & carousel with tiny horses
           going round
merrily on 16th Avenue across from ocean's wide
           beach —
Old ladies with rolls of fat round their waists and silk
           stockings

on boardwalk benches faced the blue water spread's
      sunny waves —
Ocean side infancy, pails in brown salt puddles of
      sandcastles
A thrill at the heart, hearing German Attack Poland
      radio, I biked to tell Esther Cohen
or Claire Mann niece of movie mogul Louis B. Mayer
      of Metro Goldwyn Mayer owned Mayfair
      Theater —
Riding under the full moon on the Ferris Wheel last
      night 40 years ago,
grabbing the brass ring from the horse riding up and
      down whirling slowly ecstatically to carousel
      toot tune
repeated, the floating balance and calm of marijuana
      meditation
Now Mindy her second daughter's alive young
      vegetarian eyes
by the ocean at Long Beach, in the run down section
      cleaned white in late May shine —
So return through the past to this moment on Route 36
      Sandy Hook to Perth Amboy
past Exxon whose gas our car burns the Rockefellers —
      David
they say wants to be loved liked respected — as long as
      he's loved and pharmacied —
I was car sick on the bus to Morristown, Naomi in
      Greystone that war year? she too afraid of
      Hitler —

my first mother a victim of persecution of Jewess crazed
        by Earth Electric
Meanwhile I went to the shore every year from 1935 till
        World War II
when I went to High School and campaigned for Irving
        Abramson for Congress
& lost to Congressman Gordon Canfield Republican
        Isolationist
I write newsletters to Paterson papers, thirteen years
        old saved vast clipping pix of Hitler and
        Hindenburg blow up
Claire whirling away at dances with her boyfriends, a
        normal Jewish crowd
that went to showers and proms. When I think of the
        bodies chill graves coffins & absence —
Then Claire grew up and got married to Jerry Gorlin
        and moved to the ocean library in Rumsen,
        NJ —
Cornell Hospital later rosey on the bed, hair cut for
        cancer therapy, I gave her a Buddhabook —
Sudden hearted Death, old Claire young cousin Claire
Louis, Rose, and Claire, names returning from Belmar
        through Perth Amboy and the Raritan River
        Bridge, outlooking Raritan Bay
— distant towers of World Trade Center, passing White
        Gas tanks flat on the marshes of Linden
Watercastles and barber-striped transmission towers
        electric-armed with wires
& smokestacks smelling industrial not far from Louis

graveyard
Cracker stacks and flues & ironstairwayed metal tubes
      smoking at Elizabeth's border
& the big brown gas tanks sinking into earth on their
      skeleton struts —
Newark airport, insurance buildings at left hand New
      York's skein of towers resting on the right
      horizon
Railroad *Southern* red cars under Jersey City's red-brick
      church, green-copper spiked under blue sky
Look how bright Manhattan! towery below the hill, car
      graveyard by the Turnpike,
Higher than Empire State
Mayor Hague's Hospital, scandals not run properly
      my Grandmother didn't like the way she was
      treated.
Past the Exxon sign thru Holland Tunnel's bathroom-
      polished tile
    Good old N.Y. cobblestoned and sunny

                    —May 20, 1978

Published in: *American Poetry Review,* vol. 8, no. 3 (May/June
1979), p. 26.

A Brief Praise Of Anne's Affairs

She was born in Greenwich Village
She saw Gregory Corso ambling
    by MacDougal Street looking for an angry fix
She has a mother who translates
    the Greek poets including Sikelianos
She has affairs with Poets & Poetesses,
    Novelists, Bards & Carpenters
She has affairs with international
    Shamanic minstrels dancing naked
She has affairs with herself on the side
    like anybody else
She sits & meditates & prostrates
She has affairs with books
    she writes, publishes, copulates
    gives birth to books
She's been around the world to
    Amsterdam and Kathmandu
She comes back & has affairs with
    Buddha inside out in 10 directions
She goes away again like a
    princess covered
    with diamonds & has affairs
    with sapphires
    emeralds, amber & rubies

She had an affair w/ the ancient
    Christian Church St. Marks in the
    Bowery lasting a decade till
    the church burned down
She has affairs with William S.
    Burroughs when he isn't
    looking and when he is
    looking
She edits Full Court Books
    like a basketball queen
She coordinates the J.K. School
    of Disembodied Poetics with
    her left pinkie and a
    nervous breakdown full
    of personal perfumo
She sings Contralto verses
    like a 19th century opera
    star
She orates her vowels like an
    owl, she whistles consonants
    like a fragile canary
She flies over her house in
    Boulder like an eagle
She's friends with Andrei
    Voznesensky, Chögyam Trungpa
    & Bob Dylan
She belongs in the White House
    surrounded by coke-sniffing
    Vajrayana bureaucrats

She eats she sleeps she shits &
    pisses with ordinary mind
She teaches Apprentices
    how to listen like Plato
She knocks me out, she thrills
    my bones, she supports my
    skull with her right hand
She's the Muse of Naropa
She's 80 years old in Ted Berrigan's
    whitehaired mind
She's Anne Waldman

—August 2, 1978

Published in: *Possible Flash,* no. 1 (1979), pp. 17–18.

Popeye and William Blake Fight to the Death

(by Kenneth Koch and Allen Ginsberg)

[Note: Ginsberg's lines are in bold.]

Popeye sat upon his chair,
Reading William Blake.
Blake got up and screamed out there,
"This seaman is a fake."

I as William Blake complained
Of Popeye reading me.
William Blake could not attain
My great Popeye sublimity.

William Blake sat there and stared,
At Popeye's bulging muscle.
William Blake had never dared,
To engage him in a tussle.

Mary Blake however, sat,
Right next to Olive Oil,
And cooked her spinach in a pot,
In fact was Mary's foil.

Mary Blake washed underwear,
While Sweetpea crawled about.
Mary Blake she wept a tear,
And Sweetpea gave a shout.

//

Mary Blake in London town,
Said, "Why is Popeye present?
I think I'll walk old Bill around
And try to shoot a pheasant."

Mary Blake on Primrose Hill,
Saw Alice called the goon,
Wonderland it was presumed,
To see the beast so soon.

Mary Blake's apocalypse,
Popeye's Deuteronomy,
Made her kiss Bill on the lips,
And praise his male economy.

Bill and Mary sat down nude
And tried to read the Bible.
Mr. Stothard came in rude,
And acting rather trodled

Mary Blake said "Popeye, there,
Sweetpea and Olive Oil,
Please throw Stothard through the air",
Popeye began to boil.

Mr. Stothard was a friend,
of Popeye and the Blakes,

Wandering wall-eyed through the streets,
Your rhymes are somewhat fake

Stothard, he could never rhyme
And he could never spell,
William Blake both at one time,
Could do it rather well.

William Blake a vision had,
Of Popeye high ascending.
For Milton was that little lad,
With Heaven's azure blending.

William Blake said, "Milton sir,"
And Popeye answered "Dearest."
Please come back to earth bestir,
For earth is quite the clearest.

Milton floating in the air,
was really Popeye reader.
Said however, "I am there",
Then Blake declared a battle dire
On Milton and his spirit
And he threw Popeye in the fire
You'd think that that would clear it.

But Popeye rose a stronger man,
The modern spirit lighting.

And closed the Blake up in a can,
On nightmares they were riding.

Then Popeye cried, "I've won the battle."
And Blake said "Down the shade,"
And Olive said, "You've quite a clout,"
And Mary stayed unlaid.

Somehow our subject ought to be
The battle of these Titans.
However Allen as you see,
We haven't got to the fightin'.

There has been combat old and new,
And yet what was the issue?
Something to do with shades and you,
And Olive frail as tissue.

Something to do with Blake's foresight
And Sweetpea's backward looking.
Something to do with Mary's fright,
And Olive's awful cooking.

Milton entered in the air,
And flew above the comics.
Blake in the morass floundered there,
And wrote on many topics.

//

Thus we end the contest new,
Which Padgett has suggested.
Thus the last line given to you,
We don't know who was bested.

—St. Mark's Poetry Project, New York, May 9, 1979

Unpublished.

For School Kids In New Jersey

Dawn I've been up all night answering letters
— Now to write a poem for 360 child poets:
Don't grow up like me, you never get enough sleep!
It's 6 AM, my friends are arguing, crying in the kitchen
Sausages are smoking on the stove, the poor pigs,
Taxis are passing down Avenue A to work
Buses are grinding down the street empty
Birds are twittering on the church steeple, cats
                              yowling in the alley,
Punk Rock's already playing on the phonograph
— It's Thursday October 4th, time to go to bed.

—New York, October 4, 1979

Published in: *Wit and Whimsy,* vol. 2 (June 19, 1980), p. 3.

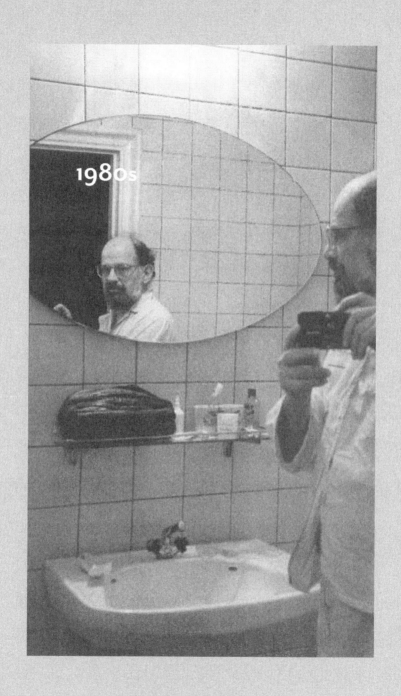

1980s

Second Spontaneous Collaboration Into the Air, Circa 23 May 1980
(by Ted Berrigan and Allen Ginsberg)

Playing tapes of Woody Guthrie singing "Dust-
    Pneumonia Blues"
We drove two hours across sun-baked pleasant hilly
    Oklahoma landscape
Chatting about the latest war propaganda news
In a red Ford, rich man's car & all the gossip we could
    scrape

Up from the sandstone ruins of Arlo's father's hillside
    house —
Bearing freshly removed gifts, shingle nails, to take
    back to New York City friends
We sat awhile, stood awhile, scratched our heads, &
    searched out a little mouse
It wasn't a mouse, it was a man from Wisconsin, who'd
    also come to see Woody's house! Then

I walked by myself down the dirt alley & saw a shack
    where no one lived with a large TV
And when I rose from meditation you led us down the
    mockingbird lane & showed that shack to me
An old grey-haired woman eating peanuts out of her
    hand & putting them into her mouth

Came through the screen-door onto the porch to feed
    her cat while we stood looking south

We snapped our photographs in Oklahoma looking
    downhill on the plains
There were four of us & now we're gone & Woody's
    house remains.

—May 23, 1980

Published in: *United Artists,* no. 11 (September 1980), p. 28.

A Tall Student

A tall student
walks down the mall
in full moonlight
passing silent window displays
where naked mannequin
observes her fingernails

—*Boulder, CO, ca. July 1980*

Unpublished.

[Poem]

Good God I got high bloodpressure answering
letters from Germany, Argentina, France!
I should meditate under the clouds again.

—ca. December 1980

Unpublished.

Amnesiac Thirst For Fame

An "autograph hound" armed
with a golden platter and a
  gun
kneeled before John and
  killed the Beatles.

A stringy-haired artist
tiptoed thru St. Peter's
and unsculpted
  Michelangelo's
polished marble elbow with a
  hammer,
Christ defenseless lying in his
  stone Mama's arms.

Staring out of the canvas
  under their Feathered Hats
Rembrandt's Night Watchers
were blind to the Slasher
that tore thru their coats with
  a razor.

Did someone steal Mona
  Lisa's smile forever from
  the Louvre?

—ca. December 8, 1980

Published in: *Rolling Stone,* no. 335 (January 22, 1981), p. 70.

[Poem]

A knock, look in the mirror
    "Reagan's been shot"
The click of the door.

—Boulder, CO, March 30, 1981

Published in: *Shearsman,* no. 7 ([first quarter] 1982), p. 31.

The Black Man

                    in shiny
leather cap and neat jacket
held up his aluminum splint
            bandaged finger
Shouting to the subway tunnel's tile walls
        "Dirty Nigger! Dirty Nigger!"
    all the platform's length
            under 14th Street —
Continued grieving crosstown
    "Dirty Nigger! Dirty Nigger!"
            through the crowded car
till the last stop, "Shut up!
    Shut up!" at the exit door
        a half-white lady hissed
And far down the 8th Avenue platform's
        forest of iron pillars
            "Dirty Nigger! Dirty Nigger!"
                    still echoed —
Climbing the subway stairs
        I still heard the distant
    "Dirty Nigger" voice as I walked

42d Street underground
to the Port Authority Bus Terminal

—*New York, March 30, 1981*

Published in: *American Poetry Review,* vol. 14, no. 6 (November/
December 1985), p. 16.

Thundering Undies
(by Allen Ginsberg and Ron Padgett)

Passing through Manhattan's sodium vapor sidestreet
      glare
with pink electric powderpuffs overhead,
mmmmm, that Catholic churchwall's old as Science
tho Science is older, but O please don't tell me about it
      tonight,
no pain please in the strange spring light,
tho my baby's waiting on the corner with 160 pounds of
      meat
on her 148 bones all for sale for 25 bucks.
Furious & Aurelius, now that we're back in town, tell her
to take cosmetics from the air, and let the dark blue city
sift slowly down to where lamplight shadows her cheeks
& her lips shine dayglo purple moist with sperm of her
      300 adorers
— O come let us adore her, weird Madonna of the street
and not in real great shape, though we're in far-off
      Elsewhere
with our sad souls and aching teeth! Too late for old
      loves,
but a little nosegay of pansies cut by Time's tractor
      where
the pasture meets the dirt road and my heart meets the
      flower bed

dug up years ago to make East 12th Street, where you
        float
a little off the ground, thinking of the withered posy of
        pussy-
willows cox-stamens & rosepetal lips dumped in the
        garbage can
by unthinking lovers I used to sleep & giggle with,
crazed, hateful & disappointed, Catullus.

—April 21, 1981

Published in: *Mag City*, no. 12 (1981), p. 16.

Trungpa Lectures

Now that bow arrow brush & fan are balanced in the
   hand
— What about a glass of water? —
Holding my cock to pee, the Atlantic gushes out.
Sitting down to eat, Sun and Moon fill the plate.

—July 8, 1981

Published in: *Mag City*, no. 12 (1981), p. 15.

Pinsk After Dark
(by Ted Berrigan and Allen Ginsberg)

Reborn a rabbi in Pinsk, reincarnated backward time
I gasped thru my beard full of mushroom barley soup;
two rough-faced blonde Cossacks, drinking wine,
paid me no heed, not remembering their futures —
 Verlaine & Rimbaud.

—February 12, 1982

Published in: Anne Waldman, ed., *Nice to See You: Homage to Ted Berrigan* (Coffee House Press, 1991), p. 116.

Two Scenes
(by Ted Berrigan and Allen Ginsberg)

Time Mag's Central American Expert sd
    Gen. Haig was "an asshole" —
What a surprise in private on the telephone,
    we dated each other up for next Thursday.

I stood outside the Kiev tonight, nose pressed
    to the plate glass, feet freezing
in city mush, and watched two aging lovers
    inhale their steaming bowls of mushroom barley
        soup.

—February 12, 1982

Published in: Anne Waldman, ed., *Nice to See You: Homage to Ted Berrigan* (Coffee House Press, 1991), p. 118.

Listening To Susan Sontag

All the Centuries are the same.
Up to date, fashionably dressed in
     skin, hair, worm mucous,
     bark & feather
Fire burns continuously in the
     hearth pit
warmth beats thru hearts,
     footsteps walk to the grave
     hole
or pass out the cemetery at the
     low gate in the iron fence

to the grocery store on the hill,
     Chautauqua Meadows
     past caves & pine woods to the
     mountain wall Flatironed
     against blue space
Clouds float above
as sailed over Jurassic
     Dinosaur heads lifted staring
     higher than palm fronds
at the shining wall where Michael
     stands on the gate house arch
     with brilliant sword

waiting to usher in the next
    Millennia's five billion
    skulls.
Amazed Generation! Found Generation!
    Diamond Generation! Brainwashed
    Generation! Amnesiac
    T.V. Bureaucracy Voidoids!
New Wave Punk Generation!
    Neutron Bomb blast Babies!
    Apocalypse Spermatozoa!
Did you grow up imbibing
    Microchip sex waters?
Will you marry me in the
    next Millennium?
Must I wait for the Great Year?
The only thing different Century
    after Century
is the sun rises in a different
    Fish or Water Pot
    every two Millennia!
But that's already happened 167,000 times!

—April 22, 1982

Published in: *City*, vol. 1, no. 9 (1984), pp. 61–62.

You Want Money?

You want money?
fill out the forms
the universe will unroll its endless bank notes at this
        majestic stroke of your pen
money from Chilean coal miners' sweat in Loda
        mineshafts
money from whales' ambergris
opium clipper ship profits from Indochina
luckor laundered by the CIA through the Buck Rogers
        Foundation in the 21st century
peace money plucked from Venezuela by Chase Bank
pouring black gold on Wall Street
What?
yours for the asking
all the empty diamonds of South Africa
multi-national sapphires
blue oceans of desire
emeralds dragged up from Amazon River bottom by Mr.
        Ludwig and U.S. Steel
Ford's amber pennies,
Rockefeller's oily rubies red as boy's blood in Bolivia
walk off with the treasury building under your left arm
        like a kiddie bank on Market Street
pick up the Federal Reserve and put it in your back

pocket
paper money, thin as dreams
take a wasted tree write your own tender
sign your own name as if you were a Secretary of the
        Treasury
this suffering money comes from nowhere, goes
        nowhere
this unborn money's made by labor millions who cut
        coastal forests
sucking oil up in Evanston Wyoming
dredging uranium on gold peninsulas aboriginal
        preserve
burning electric to fuel book sights for pots and pans
        that bit your ears off in Santiago
rob the bank and scatter money back to the trees and
        fields and mountains
spend on art with ever returning agronomy
beautiful speech, practical windmills
children's meditative pencils
nightsoil recycled to daylit meadows
walnut forests green shade legible flowers
hazel nut shaded city streets
labor intensive persimmons near the Great Lakes' clear
        blue.

—Boulder, CO, April 28, 1982

Unpublished.

Cats Scratching

Cats scratching my leg, nails in my raw skin,
pulling at wool pants' threads —
Shall I sit here dignified & let you scratch me to Death
or rise from my chair, angry, at war with white kittens?

—ca. April 1982

Published in: John Castlebury, ed., *Windhorse* (Samurai Press, July
1982), p. 50.

[Poem]

I used to live in gay sad Paris!
Decades in taxi-honk New York!
Smelly London, watery Venice,
Bright Tanger, and dark Benares!
Now I meditate in the mountains.

—Boulder, CO, May 1982

Published in: Karel Appel, *Street Art* (H.J.W. Becht, 1985), p. 249.

[Poem]

As the rain drips from the gutter on to the bushes of
       the imperial court lawn
And a motorcycle putters up Cascade Avenue
The ice cream man having delivered his sandwiches
The poets began to consider their minds

      — *The Drawing Room, the Kalapa Court, Boulder, CO,*
                              July 26, 1982

Published in: *Friction,* vol. 1, no. 2/3 (Winter [February 27, 1983]
1982), p. 82.

[Poem]

Having bowed down my forehead on the pavement on
      Central Park West
By the car wheels of the guru
Whose vehicle I had once stolen in the presence of my
      father
Having taken a vow to be his love-slave
For this and other lifetimes, if any
Having been humiliated in my Ginsberg-hood and
      praised for the same Ginsberg-hood
I accept the homage of my teacher-pupil and remain
      with my forehead on the pavement at his feet.

— The Drawing Room, the Kalapa Court, Boulder, CO,
July 26, 1982

Published in: *Friction,* vol. 1, no. 2/3 (Winter [February 27, 1983]
1982), p. 84.

Far Away

They say Blacks work sweating
in hot mines thousands of feet
deep in mountains of South Africa
to bring up gold & diamonds shining
on earth into the hands of White
bankers, politicians, police & armies.

—November 8, 1982

Published in: *American Poetry Review,* vol. 14, no. 6 (November/
December 1985), p. 16.

Back To Wuppertal

  Back to Wuppertal
in a car, thru snowy forests
  Belgium to Köln and
the highway filled with trans-European trucks
  Peter barefoot
his toes on the dashboard, I was
  humming
base thump parts to "Airplane Blues"
Steven reading Lennon's last conversa-
  tion in a book
— Jurgen Schmidt in his silk foulard
  sparkled with sequins
driving & thinking, "Netherlands fields
  pass by, I stay;
I pass by, Netherlands fields remain"
and threw up his right hand remembering
  he just thought that.

                                    —February 4, 1983

Published in: Joachim Ortmanns and Wolfgang Mohrhenn, eds.,
Allen Ginsberg on Tour February 16, 1983 (Lichtblick Video, 1983).

Am I A Spy From The Moon?

Am I a Spy from the moon?
    a lunar Communist?
A Capitalist Counterrevolutionary
    from the land of Big Prick?
No I just wandered in from
    the Buddhafields
for a cup of bloody tea.

—*Wuppertal, West Germany, February 16, 1983*

Published in: *United Artists* (1983), p. 100.

[Poem]

Awakened at dawn trying to run away —
   Got caught dream
     shop-lifting

—August 1983

Published in: *Notebook,* no. 3 (April 1984), p. 4.

[Poem]

Grey clouds hang over
            Flatirons

Boulder hangs under
                    sky —

Brown leaves fall down

—November 1, 1983

Published in: *Daily Camera* (November 20, 1983), Sunday Camera
Magazine section, p. 1.

1/29/84 N.Y.C.

Up late Sunday, late nite reading thru New York Times
Danced slow motion Tai Chi once,
boiled water, hot lemonade purifies the liver
Twice more the 13 steps of Tai Chi,
cleaned my face, teeth, altar in my bedroom,
filled seven brass cups with water & laid them out
        straight rowed
Sat for an hour — Why'd the *New York Times* call Living
        Theatre riffraff?
Has CIA taken over culture? am I a mad bohemian with
        bad bile?
The steamheat radiator burned down ancient forests,
my window was open, excess heat escaped
I could hear chattering & cries of children
from the church steps across the street —
well dressed adults stepped out fur collared
as I looked up from my pillow —
hundreds of fluffy snowflakes filled the air
above East 12th Street's lamps & cars

floating down like dandelion seeds from grey sky
floating up and drifting west and east by the fire escape.

—New York, January 29, 1984

Published in: Alan Moore and Josh Gosciak eds., *A Day in the Life.* (Evil Eye Books, 1990), pp. 132–133.

CXXV

Surviving death,
Feminine-jawed Williams: grey Rutherford house-gable
       Tara, Quan Yin, Kannon
       "Same eyes as an Indian holyman"
            Avelokiteshvara
       whose fingers touched the window on Ridge
       Road
               "There's a lot of Bastards out there."
Bunting stands on a marble floor, my *Kaddish?*
                "Too many words. . ."
Sd the *Newcastle Times* Financial Editor
       on marble lobby floor
   "Salutations dear Bunting, I'm leaving for yr
       Istanbool"
           So, blond hair to shoulder, Newcastle Tom
           Pickard
               snapped his photo

                        —ca. April 1984

Published in: *Unmuzzled Ox,* vol. 12, no. 2 (issue 24) (1986), p. 17.

Rose Is Gone

Rose is gone
from Stuyvesant Town
died when I was away
        92 years old —
my mother's Communist friend
            Rose Savage
— died a couple years ago
When I was teaching in Buddhaland —
      She had Man Ray paintings
           on her wall
and my mother Naomi screamed for her
at 288 Graham Avenue in 1937
      thinking the Murderers were
           at large
— Then I got mad at her defending Stalin
      when she was old half deaf, her voice cracked
           white handed in her apartment —
vegetables, nuts, bananas and carrots —
      a little boiled chicken — in her ice box
She couldn't get around after 1978
couldn't walk to the Safeway.
        //

II

Where's Rose? Where's Naomi?
Where's our old apartment
on East 7th Street?

—*June 24, 1984*

Published in: *Camp Kerouac Summer '84* (Jack Kerouac School of
Disembodied Poetics Summer Writing Program/Naropa Institute,
July 1984), p. 40.

[Poem]

3'd day down Yangtze River, yesterday
passed vast mountain gorges and hairpin
river-bends, mist sun and cement factory
soft coal dust everywhere, all China
got a big allergic cold. Literary dele-
gation homebound after 3 weeks, now I'm
traveling separately like I used to — except
everywhere omnipresent kindly Chinese
Bureaucracy meets me at airports & boats
& takes me to tourist hotels & orders meals. I'm
trying to figure a way out — envious of 2
bearded hippies traveling 4th class in
steerage eating tangerincs & bananas —
sleepers in passageways on mats, Chinese
voyagers playing checkers. Saw Beijing,
Great Wall, tombs & palaces, Suchow's
Tang gardens, Hangchow's West Lake walkway
dyke to hold the giant water in years of drought
built up by governors Tsu-Tung-Po and Po-Chu-I.
Saw Cold Mt. Temple w/ Snyder who'd
heard its bell echo across ocean.

—China, November 11, 1984

Published in: *Big Scream,* no. 20 (February 15, 1985), p. 4.

African Spirituality Will Save
the Earth

Seattle Gospel Chorus
clap hands
raise your voice
shake your ass
save the earth
Bluefields Moravian church amazing
the whiteheaded virgins dissolve in three-chord
        harmony
Praise The Lord!
Wrap around the May Pole
tears in your eyes
freedom of the body
trust the Lord the heart energy
clap your hands
have a dream in Bluefields
bow down to the imperial crown
the lone May King
too old to dance except shuffle the streets
just at the right time
nods approval, applauds the chorus

break down your empire O armed victor
animosity

—Bluefields, Nicaragua, January 29, 1986

Unpublished.

Face to Face

Face to face
with silent grace
Take your place
in the old rat race

—ca. February 1986

Published in: *Poetry Project Newsletter,* no. 119 (February 1986),
p. 7.

Who's Gone?

Edith Sitwell's gone
and Frances Waldman too
Cyril Connolly you know who
Tom Driberg far away
Lionel Trilling's gone
so's Mark Van Doren
Raymond Weaver and Professor Andrew Shapp
Kerouac Cassady Lew Welch
Poor Bobby Kaufman who lived upstairs on Second
        Street
John Lennon and Robert Kennedy
several presidents I never met
my mother Naomi, my father Louie
W.H. Auden and Chester his lover Kallman
Cannastra and Dorothy Day
Catholic Workers gone underground where worms
        make hay
many others
Rose Savage, Man Ray,
my Aunt Rose, sad Lady Day
Charlie Parker, Thelonious Monk and Martin Luther
        King still young
Ahh David Kennedy gone
Ahh Hibiscus

Kenneth Rexroth, Kenneth Patchen
young John Hoffman
so long ago, what he looked like I don't know
all these gone, I'll be gone too
Going where my old Dean McKnight went
Dwight Macdonald, and Joan Vollmer and Tom
            O'Bedlam
Ian Sommerville and Michael Portman
Jimi Hendrix and Howard Alk
if they went out how could I balk?
Jim Morrison, Janis Joplin
I never met with Charlie Chaplin
Bertrand Russell sent me a letter
I got sick and felt even better
I've tried honesty boiled in oil
digested by ego loving gargoyle
Enough, I gotta go to sleep at night all alone
I've no wife my eyes closed without the moon
I've stayed up midnight till afternoon.

                    —*Naropa, Boulder, CO, ca. May 22, 1986*

Unpublished.

Bob Dylan Touring with Grateful Dead

Bob Dylan Touring with the Grateful Dead
acid crowd federal narcs in the capitol, alert alert,
Now's their chance
Boy George already forgotten in headline video
pleads new songs even in pain
indifferent yuppie high school tank topped athletes
       shudder blonde bodies vomiting in the back seat
car crashed into an Iowa lamp pole
better not get high in the Detroit stadium naked for the
       narcs, a bust, a bust
the agricultural poet drunk in his red bikini in the
       Buddhist garden
if I feel dread, what feels he alone with his family crazy
       in outer Long Island?
Where can he go with alcohol and the landlord's
       eviction notice comes to us all?
gentrification will oust us from our nest
where put books and file cabinets heavy with paper gold?
Wake, smoke another cigarette with aching back
the last in breath through cancered throat
too late to go back to college a smokeless virgin
lead a purist spotless life of commercial crime
unfair, an 80-year old stepmother's bride broods in her
       garden apartment

who'll change the light bulb,
climb up on the ladder and fix the triumph of death on
      the wall?
Have I learned the *Book Of The Dead* in time?
breathing Manhattan's springtime
bomb Libya,
Ukrainian wheat crop poisoned by radioactive burst
whispers in the UN corridors 70th floor
the Secretary General sees a black cloud approach
over Queens and Brooklyn in a hundred years
down the street Gregory tokes a joint by Dag
      Hammarskjöld's private bus stop
the driver smelt incense, out into the kiosk he whispered
      to the supervisor
What's that smell? Is that a police patrol by the fire
      hydrant?
Where will the drunken farmer go if they kick him out
      of the Buddhist retreat?
the sky turned black
dread heaven over Columbia Library dome
and later in the bookstore, animal clerks glared
      wounded behind the cash register
skeletons standing in place behind the counters and
      shelves
filled with Plotinus and Sir Thomas Aquinas.

—ca. May 22, 1986

Unpublished.

1990s

Asia Minor for Gregory

Sunset, a marble tea table on Kusadasi's
    hotel yacht harbor, I remembered
a stork flapped wings upward meeting atop one
    ragged column
left of old Cybele's Artemisium at Ephesus, favorable
    omen;
Halicarnassus' mausoleum a wonder vanished from
    Bodrum's coast
a million glass shards left over, shipwrecked six
    Moslem centuries past;
The Pythian Oracle's Divinity fled Didyma to
    Earth's bowels early in the last millennium,
At sunset Apollo's columns echo with
    the bawl of one God;
Looking for words at Pergamum, only
    a one-walled shell
stands on a peaktop over plain,
Hippocrates' library shipped to Alexandria long
    ago
Zeus and Diana's marble loins raptured to
    London Paris & Berlin;
Musician & poet sit silent on a long stone
    bench in fig tree shade

with Croesus above Aphrodesia's weedy
 Stadium
Go roar thru sulphurous dawn's rosy haze
 heavenward over Homer's odorous Smyrna
to meet United States of America's Jewish
 Ambassador to Ankara.

—8 a.m., June 29, 1990

Unpublished.

[Poem]

The moon in the dewdrop is the real moon
The moon in the sky's an illusion
Which Madhyamaka school does that represent?

—Rocky Mountain Dharma Center, CO, August 1991

Published in: *Shambhala Sun,* vol. 1, no. 5 (January/February 1993), p. 57.

New Years Greeting
(for Ron Padgett)

It is a beauteous evening calm and free
Spanish voices on Our Lady Help of Xtians steps
a new year's come, eternity & I can't eat baloney
& avoiding any salt probably can't drink Schweppes.

You got to hand it to the Doctor's Hospital
Your heart your liver kidneys and arteriosclerosis
Fortunately sick going in I came out well
Before my time the threat of Death a nosy gnosis

This can't go on forever short of breath weak heart
Wasn't my fault don't drink don't drive don't smoke
don't stir sugar in my coffee don't you start
up with me 'bout eating bacon sniffing coke

I could have suffocated didn't but live on
upon this earth I walk and eat and write this poem to
      Ron.

—*New York, 2 a.m., January 4, 1992*

Published in: *The Northern Centinel,* vol. 205, no. 4 (Fall 1993), p. 8.

Hermaphrodite Market

I bought a
pretty boy
at the her-
maphrodite
market and
lived happily
ever after.

I sold a
sweet thing
at the her-
maphrodite
market &
went home
happy.

—May 2, 1994

Published in: *Ma!*, no. 7 (ca. 1994), front cover.

Last Conversation with Carl
or In Memoriam

[re: Twin Towers Explosion on TV]
    Carl: It's a real turn-on
to be well and functioning
in the middle of the mess.
It's hard to find
anything real because
the physical thing
changes so quickly
you don't know which way to turn
because...I'm incontinent
...don't know the proper way
to behave...
    I hope my suffering
doesn't last too long.
    So maybe pneumonia
will do it in like my mom
    Pain I haven't had
to deal with much
lately... they've got
me on the anti pain...
    and they also insist
on the oxygen which
is no longer too meaningful

to me. No longer
   effective
I feel like my mother's
way — go off into pneumonia
and heart failure… but
my heart is too damn
strong…
   **Allen: What do
you think death is?**
   Carl: Death is a fading away —
which I'd like to go easily
like my mother… imitate
my mother… this last
year of grace has been
excessive — I just want
to get it over with —
   I just want to say a
few words about (the literary scene
of) Kerouac Burroughs
   There's not much more
for me to say anyway, but
it's been a lot of fun
   At that time it was
very exciting to me —
   I wasn't that mad,
I was intellectually adventurous
and interested myself in Artaud and
I was a loner — even
in my own family circles

I was a loner — intellectual
eccentric — How much
recognition I got from
my family? I got very little
I guess. (coughing)
It's like strangulation...
      As who'll take me back to my room
      For a while I was very
serious about surrealism —
It was just another movement
I was serious about these
movements —
      **Allen: Do you feel I did the wrong
      thing putting the spotlight on you
      by using your name in "Howl"?**
      Carl: You gave me my first
outlet in *Neurotica* — for
some recognition... I guess
it went to my head
      The life I spent was all right
I'm dying of lung cancer
an unusual thing — can't
bother to figure it out.
      Too bad if I was foolish,
it won't matter much much
longer. I hope I
get out without too
much agony. For my mother
it was nice, she just waved

waved good-by.

I was there before
she died... (then) they notified
me about my mother

Then I felt my repson-
sibility was really over.

I spent the next year
just wandering about...
until this

It was a wonderful
year — wonderful and
meaningless with
my mother gone... I had
no responsibility... I had
a girlfriend Elaine... now
she claims she loves me...
marry me, all kinds of
things —

**Allen: Kerouac stuck by his
mother**

Carl: "Boys and their mothers"

The beats were kind of a
Cosmopolitan grouping, some from
the suburbs, some from the
inner city, and some people
wanted to be beats, some were
real beats, some made believe they
were and they weren't.

A mid-century

Cold War hang-up . . .

So I'm still somewhat
reluctant to say good-bye —
I don't know why I'm
hanging on so desperately...
It's just hard to let
go... you hang on
with a kind of bulldog
rapacity ... I suppose
like people being executed...
the animal in it is still
                    there
Carl to Allen: except
...you're really
looking good...
You look younger
to me — spirits are young —
Rabbi was here — He said
he'd pray for me...That's
about it...The Jewish
thing is OK — I let it
pass...This is a formal
social status — against
which I make no challenge...
Back in room, with oxygen
mask.
Allen: Does it help?
Carl: it relieves me a little,
makes it a little better.

(Carl volunteered)...One thing that
still interests me is sex
(gestures towards his lap)
   I looked at him grizzled
and thin, but calm, seemed to've
gained strength, up on pillow
bed head raised a bit so he
wasn't flat, a bed by window
in a two man room, other bed
leathery and empty.
   **Allen: You mean even now, you have
enuf strength to be interested
                  in that?**
   Carl: Yes... my last sex was with...
8 months ago — I had
the strength & acquitted
myself adequately. So I feel
I'd fulfilled my last respon-
sibility.

                    — *VA Hospital, Bronx, NY, February 26, 1993*

Published in: *Poetry Project Newsletter,* vol. 149 (April/May 1993),
pp. 6–7.

Dream of Carl Solomon

I meet Carl Solomon.
"What's it like in the afterworld?"

"It's just like in the mental hospital.
You get along if you follow the rules."

"What are the rules?"

"The first rule is: Remember you're dead.
The second rule is: Act like you're dead."

—ca. 1996

Published in: Marc Olmsted, *Don't Hesitate: Knowing Allen Ginsberg* (Beatdom Books, 2004).

Acknowledgments

I am deeply grateful to many people and institutions who helped with the compilation of the poems for this book. Peter Hale at the Allen Ginsberg Trust offered constant support and encouragement through the years from inception to final publication. Without his tireless energy and extraordinary efforts this volume simply would not exist.

The people at the Wylie Agency, Jeff Posternak in particular, brought the book to the attention of Grove Atlantic. The team at Grove under the leadership of Morgan Entrekin included Peter Blackstock and Judy Hottensen and they have seen the book through the publication process, producing this beautiful work for Ginsberg's readers. Allen would have been as happy to work with them as I was.

Heartfelt appreciation goes out to the many people who helped locate and track down various lost texts. Among them Gordon Ball, David Cope, Elsa Dorfman, Bill Gargan, Rachel Homer, Bill Keogan, Ella Longpre, Sterling Lord, Kaye McDonough, Tim Moran, Marc Olmsted, Peter Orlovsky, Simon Pettet, Gary Snyder, John Tytell, Anne Waldman, and Sylvia Whitman deserve special recognition.

Thanks, too, to libraries nationwide, who have carefully preserved Ginsberg's texts in a wide variety of formats. The libraries at Columbia University, Stanford University, and the University of North Carolina each contain major collections of Ginsberg material. Polly Armstrong, Michael Basinski (University of Buffalo), Claudia Funke, Patricia Hults (Rensselaer Polytechnic Institute), Annette Keogh, Monika Lehman, Nan Mehan, Kathleen Monahan, Karla Nielsen, Tim Noakes, Michael Ryan, Jane Siegel, Aaron Smithers, Mattie Taormina, and Jocelyn Wilk helped with specific items.

Portions of this work have appeared in the following publications, and the Allen Ginsberg Trust is grateful to all of them: *American Poetry Review, Beatitude, Big Scream, Big Sky, Bombay Gin, Chicago Review, City, City Lights Journal, Clothesline, Columbia Jester, Columbia Review, Coyote's Journal, Daily Camera, Damascus Road, Eastside Mirror, Embers, End, Fag Rag, Ferret, Friction, Fuck You: A Magazine of the Arts, Great Society, High Times, La Huerta, Ma!, Mag City, Marrahwannah Quarterly, Northern Centinel, Notebook, Poetry Newsletter, Poetry Project Newsletter, Poets at Le Metro, Portage, Possible Flash, Rolling Stone, Seven Days, Shambhala Sun, Shearsman, Spectrum, Strike Newspaper, Synapse, Tax Talk, United Artists, Unmuzzled Ox, Villager, Voices, Washington Post, Wit and Whimsy,* and *Yugen.*

And last but never least, Judy Matz has remained steadfast in her support of this work and this editor for more than forty years. To her I dedicate this and all my efforts.

Notes

1940s

Rep Gordon Canfield

In the fall of 1942 Republican incumbent Gordon Canfield (1898–1972) ran for reelection in New Jersey's Eight Congressional District. It was Ginsberg's home district and the sixteen-year-old Allen helped campaign for the Democratic nominee, Irving Abramson, who lost to Canfield.

We leave the youthful pennants and the books,

This poem was selected as the class poem for Ginsberg's Eastside High School in Paterson, New Jersey. At his twenty-fifth high school reunion in 1968 Ginsberg read his poem again and commented: "Oh well, there it is. Doesn't seem to be much change in the world after twenty-five years."

A Night in the Village

After Ginsberg arrived at Columbia College in 1943 he began to frequent Greenwich Village with his new friends: Lucien Carr, William S. Burroughs, David Kammerer, and Jack Kerouac. This poem may reflect on common moments they shared as they visited the neighborhood bars looking for new experiences.

As Robert Genter wrote in "'I'm Not His Father': Lionel Trilling, Allen Ginsberg, and the Contours of Literary Modernism" in *College Literature,* vol. 31, no. 2 (Spring 2004): "In poems such as 'A Night in the Village' Ginsberg paid strict attention to the length of his poetic line and the closeness of his rhymes. But while he followed the New Critics in their concern with the ideological and political claims attached to poetry by liberals and communists alike and the theoretical arrogance of science which subordinated the little details of human existence to the strictures of categorical claims, Ginsberg began to reject their intense focus on form as the only source of the poetic transcendence of everyday life."

Epitaph for a Suicide; Epitaph for a Poet

Only a week after Lucien Carr (1925–2005), a close friend of Ginsberg, killed his gay stalker, David Kammerer (1911–1944), Allen wrote these two poems. Originally the first poem was titled "Epitaph for David Kammerer," but to hide the identities of the people involved Ginsberg renamed it "Epitaph for a Suicide" even though his death was far from suicide. This is the first time the two poems have been published together.

Behold! The Swinging Swan

This poem was included in a letter Ginsberg wrote to his friend Jack Kerouac. Some of the lines later turned up in a collaborative poem the two wrote called "Pull My Daisy."

1950s

Her Engagement

Following William Carlos Williams's suggestion that he look to his prose for poetic inspiration, Ginsberg went back to his journals, rearranging many passages into verse. This prose journal description of a dream was created in 1952, but reappeared as a poem in 1955.

What's buzzing

This poem was written while Ginsberg was living in San Jose with Carolyn and Neal Cassady. Unbeknownst to Carolyn was the fact that Allen and Neal were having a sexual relationship behind her back.

Thus on a Long Bus Ride; *We rode on a lonely bus*

In late December 1954, Ginsberg met Peter Orlovsky (1933–2010), the young man who became his life's companion. While living in San Francisco the two took many bus trips together, one of which must have occasioned this earlier memory. Allen liked it enough to include it in a letter to Jack Kerouac, and then reworked it for publication in *Yugen*. Both versions are included here.

There's nobody here

Carolyn Cassady kicked Ginsberg out of the house when she caught him in bed with her husband, but Neal frequently visited Ginsberg in his San Francisco apartment at 1010 Montgomery Street in North Beach.

On Nixon; Chain Poem

Richard Nixon was vice president under Dwight D. Eisenhower from 1953 until 1961. This poem was a collaborative effort by Ginsberg, Corso, and Kerouac. Later, in May 1979, Allen wrote the following about the poem. "This poem was written in a bar on Broadway near 110th Street Manhattan, soon after the Vice-President's celebrated Checkers Speech, at a time when Kerouac was besieged by *Esquire, Vogue* or other slick magazines to write "timely" articles on subjects editors thought modish. On this visit he had refused to write a "critique of American women," and said with a wry world-weary cry, "We ought to make 1500 dollars right now, write a big attack on American Women!" By applying some literary detective work, it appears that this poem must have been written either in late 1956 when the three were in Mexico City or in early 1957 before Corso left for Europe. Nixon's Checkers speech was given in 1952, but

Allen didn't meet Lafcadio until 1955, so Allen has mistaken the date.

The Real Distinguished Thing

Ginsberg was given the anesthesia laughing gas or nitrous oxide on several visits to the dentist during the late 1950s. He said that it was the first time he really felt that life was just an illusion. In later years he said that laughing gas helped turn him into a Buddhist.

1960s

To Frank O'Hara & John Ashbery & Kenneth Koch

While on a trip to South America, Ginsberg tried to interest Lawrence Ferlinghetti in publishing some of the New York School poets he knew. Here he composed a poem in their style.

Ayahuasca—

Ginsberg defined ayahuasca (*yagé* or *soga del muerto, a Banisteriopsis caapi* vine infusion used by Amazon *curanderos*) as a spiritual potion, used for medicine and sacred vision.

Walt Whitman

Ginsberg excerpted this poem from what he called "a longer poem on politics."

Tokyo Tower

After a lengthy trip to India, Ginsberg stopped to visit Gary Snyder and Joanne Kyger in Kyoto, Japan. On his way back to America he passed through Tokyo and spent a few days enjoying all the luxuries he had missed during his year and a half in India.

B.C. [Bob Creeley]

This poem was written shortly after Ginsberg had participated in the Vancouver Poetry Conference organized by Robert Creeley. Attached to the manuscript was a note from Allen to Creeley saying, "Battered that out last night, trying to approximate your style, the middle stanza almost makes it no?, but the last line sing-songs bad..."

War Is Black Magic

On October 30, 1963, Ginsberg joined several hundred picketers who were protesting a visit to San Francisco by Madame Nhu, the powerful wife of South Vietnam's secret police chief. Allen composed this poem then put it on a poster that he carried all day in what was his first of many demonstrations against the Vietnam War.

Journals November 22, '63

President John F. Kennedy was killed by an assassin's bullet in Dallas on November 22, 1963. Ginsberg, like most Americans, followed the events on television and wrote this poem.

Line 6: Robert McNamara (1916–2009) was the U.S. secretary of defense at the time.

In a Shaking Hand

This poem was composed while riding on Ken Kesey's bus "Furthur" back to New York City from Millbrook, New York, where they had been visiting Timothy Leary at the Hitchcock family mansion. Neal Cassady was driving the Day-Glo-colored psychedelic school bus and Allen titled it "Shaking — because the bus shook me."

Line 5: Shabda yoga is a spiritual form of yoga concerned with the power of words, sounds, and music.

Little Flower M.M. [Marianne Moore]

Ginsberg was asked to write a poem in honor of Marianne Moore's seventy-seventh birthday. At the time she was living at 260 Cumberland Street in Brooklyn, hence the references to the bridges, the Navy Yard, etc.

During the mid-sixties Ginsberg began to compose poetry while he was in the process of traveling. He often carried a portable tape recorder with him to record on the spot. "New York to San Fran" was composed in a notebook during one of his cross-country flights. It is one of the best results of that process but he never collected it into a book, perhaps due to the length.

Line 7: Adlai Stevenson II (1900–1965) was a politician who ran for president in 1952 and again in 1956. He died in London while on a diplomatic trip.

Line 58: Hudson River.

Line 99: Mauna Loa is a volcano in Hawaii.

Line 194: Otto Klemperer (1885–1973) was a German composer and conductor of classical music.

Line 204: *The Satan Bug* (1965) was the in-flight movie shown on this trip. It dealt with the theft of a dangerous virus by terrorists.

Line 239: Herbert Huncke (1915–1996), a writer and long-time friend of Ginsberg's, grew up in Chicago.

Line 274: The *Mainliner* was the airline's complimentary magazine.

Line 284: While in Benares, India, Ginsberg lived near the Dasawamedh Ghat, the steps that led down to the Ganges, frequented by pious Hindus and beggars alike.

Line 288: During the Vietnam War, Phnom Penh, Cambodia, was used by North Vietnamese troops as a staging area.

Line 299: Joliet, Ilinois, is the home of a well-known prison.

Line 322: Reference to the poet Hart Crane (1899–1932).

Lines 363–64: Reagan and Dr. Baxter were characters in the film *The Satan Bug* that he was watching on the plane.

Line 368: Although Adlai Stevenson was born in California, he was closely identified with Illinois and Ginsberg probably believed that he had been born there.

Line 389–98: Random quotes from *The Satan Bug*.

Line 485: References to the Russian poet Yevgeny Yevtushenko (b. 1932) and Lubyanka, which was the headquarters of the KGB in Moscow and served as its prison as well.

Line 486: Spoleto was the location in Italy of an international festival of the arts.

Line 492: Democrat/Republican.

Line 500: Fort Leavenworth, Kansas, is the site of a maximum security American prison.

Line 505: At one time the Potala Palace was the residence of the Dalai Lama in Lhasa, Tibet.

Line 511: John Wieners (1934–2002) was an American poet and author of *The Hotel Wentley Poems*.

Line 574: San Francisco, where Ginsberg had once lived.

Line 598: The Belvedere was a complex of Baroque buildings in Vienna.

Line 615: Charles Olson (1910–1970) was an American poet and the author of *The Maximus Poems*.

Line 650: Mount Tamalpais is the highest mountain peak in the San Francisco Bay area.

Liverpool Muse

After being expelled from Prague, Ginsberg arrived in
England, saw Bob Dylan perform, and was immediately
swallowed up by the music scene surrounding groups like
the Beatles and the Rolling Stones. He began to quote
a paraphrasing of Plato, "When the mode of the music
changes, the walls of the city shake." The new music gave him
hope that things were changing in the world for the better.

    Line 3: The Sink Club was a Liverpool jazz club that
featured the Motown sound.

    Line 16: The Yoruba are an African people.

Entering Kansas City High

In early 1966 Ginsberg and Peter Orlovsky drove back home
to New York from California via Kansas where their friend
and poet Charles Plymell had lined up several readings for
them.

Busted

On June 14, 1966, Ginsberg testified about his own drug use
before a special subcommittee of the U.S. Senate Committee
on the Judiciary. This poem reflects some of the opinions
that he shared with them.

Nashville April 8

Ginsberg and civil rights activists Martin Luther King Jr. and Stokely Carmichael spoke at the 1967 IMPACT Symposium held at Vanderbilt University on April 8.

After Wales Visitacione July 29 1967

"Wales Visitation" is considered to be one of Ginsberg's greatest poems of the period. This is a continuation of that poem written at the same time and under the effects of LSD.

Line 19: The Llanthony Valley is in southeast Wales.

Lines 50,52: Both Lord Hereford's Knob and Capel-y-ffin are in southern Wales.

Mabillon Noctambules

The title refers to a Paris metro station near where Ginsberg and his father stayed on the elder Ginsberg's first trip to Europe.

Line 1–2: Noctambules, Old Navy, and Lipp were Parisian cafés where Charles Baudelaire might have hung out.

Line 14: Guillaume Apollinaire's love affair with Marie Laurencin broke up on the Mirabeau Bridge.

Line 16: One of Tristan Tzara's favorite cafés was Deux Magots.

Line 18: Antonin Artaud (1896–1948) was a renowned French playwright and poet.

Line 19: Henri Michaux (1899–1984) was a Belgian-born poet who lived on Rue Segur.

Line 44: *Jamais,* French for "never."

Line 54: The White Queen was a café near Ginsberg's hotel at the time.

Lines 56–60: La Cloiserie des Lilas was one of Hemingway's favorite cafés and the "Great Lesbians" must certainly refer to his friends Gertrude Stein and Alice Toklas.

Genocide

Line 1: LeRoi Jones (1934–2014) was an African American poet and friend of Ginsberg's who changed his name to Amiri Baraka a few years before this poem was written.

No Money, No War

For a decade the Vietnam War was paramount in Ginsberg's mind as it was for many Americans. At one point he decided to stop paying taxes toward that war and he urged others to do the same.

1970s

May King's Prophecy

On the fifth anniversary of Ginsberg's election as the King of May by the students of Prague he was in New Haven,

Connecticut, in support of a strike organized by Yale students.

Hum! Hum! Hum!

In the winter of 1970–71 Ginsberg was asked to be one of the judges for the National Book Award for Poetry. He became enraged when his fellow judges selected Mona Van Duyn over Gregory Corso and he wrote this poem in protest.

The world's an illusion

When a group of New Jersey high school students asked Ginsberg to write a poem for their yearbook, it gave him an opportunity to exercise his wry sense of humor.

Reef Mantra

While on a reading tour to Australia with Lawrence Ferlinghetti, they stopped over in Fiji for a few days. Ginsberg composed several songs and a few short poems including this one and the next.

Postcard to D

While still in Fiji Ginsberg wrote this postcard to Bob Dylan, which took the form of a poem.

Inscribed in George Whitman's Guest Register

George Whitman (1913–2011) was the owner of Le Mistral Bookshop at 37 Rue de la Bûcherie, Paris, from 1951 until 1964. At that time he changed the name to Shakespeare and Company in honor of Sylvia Beach's bookstore of the same name.

Line 9: Jonathan Robbins was a young American poet and friend of Ginsberg.

Line 10: Brion Gysin (1916–1986) was an artist and the co-inventor with William S. Burroughs of the cut-up method of writing.

On Farm

For several years Ginsberg lived on a farm near Cherry Valley, New York. This poem was part of a letter Allen wrote to the poet Gary Snyder.

Wyoming

This poem was written in Wyoming while Ginsberg was on a Buddhist retreat with his meditation teacher Chögyam Trungpa Rinpoche.

Exorcism

This poem was really a curse on Nelson Rockefeller (1908–1979) who had been New York's wealthy governor from 1959 until December 18, 1973. His term ended just a few weeks before the poem was written.

Line 21: The Attica, New York, prison riot took place in September 1971. A total of thirteen guards and inmates were killed during the uprising. Rockefeller famously refused to visit the prison to negotiate a peaceful settlement.

Eyes Full of Pitchpine Smoke

Ginsberg owned land adjacent to Gary Snyder in the Sierra Mountains of California. Allen and Gary collaborated on this poem while Allen was building his own cabin there.

Line 6: The Greensfelders were neighbors.

Spring night four a.m.

In early May 1976, the Eighth Street Bookshop, owned by Ginsberg's friends Ted and Eli Wilentz, caught fire. A reporter taped Ginsberg's eulogy for the store, which became this poem.

Line 8: Amiri Baraka, aka LeRoi Jones.

Louis' First Night in Grave

When Ginsberg's father died he was buried in the family plot. The cemetery was in an industrial area near the Newark Airport.

Line 10: Rose Gaidemak was Allen's aunt.

Line 32: The Ginsberg family often spent summer holidays at the seaside resort of Belmar, New Jersey.

Line 58: Naomi Ginsberg was Allen's mother.

Line 73: Edith Ginsberg was Allen's stepmother and Louis Ginsberg's second wife.

Kidneystone Opium Traum

While taking medication for kidney stones Ginsberg recorded the following dream. The form of the poem was inspired by Michael Brownstein (b. 1943), a poet Allen knew from New York's Lower East Side.

Homage to Paris at the Bottom of the Barrel

Philip Lamantia (1927–2005) was a surrealist poet. Ginsberg's poem was inspired by Lamantia's work.

Verses Included In *Howl* Reading Boston City Hall

Occasionally Ginsberg tailored new lines for old poems for particular audiences. In 1978 he added these lines to his poem "Howl" for a reading he gave in Boston after the police arrested twenty-four men in Revere, Massachusetts, for making gay porn with underage boys.

No Way Back to the Past

This poem was another one based on Ginsberg's childhood memories of the summers he spent in Belmar, New Jersey.

Line 48: Ginsberg's mother, Naomi, spent a good deal of time as a mental patient in the Greystone Park Psychiatric Hospital in Morris Plains, New Jersey.

A Brief Praise of Anne's Affairs

Anne Waldman (b. 1945) is a poet and was co-director with Ginsberg of the Jack Kerouac School of Disembodied Poetics, part of the Naropa Institute in Boulder, Colorado.

Line 5: Angelos Sikelianos (1884–1951) was a Greek poet who was once nominated for the Nobel Prize.

Line 26: Waldman was also the director of the St. Mark's Poetry Project in New York between 1968 and 1978.

Lines 48–49: Andrei Voznesensky (1933–2010) was a Russian poet and longtime friend; Chögyam Trungpa (1939–1987) was Ginsberg's Buddhist meditation teacher and the head of the Naropa Institute.

Line 62: Ted Berrigan (1934–1983) was a poet and a friend of Ginsberg's and Waldman's.

Popeye and William Blake Fight to the Death

From time to time Ginsberg collaborated with other poets. On several occasions he and poet Kenneth Koch spontaneously exchanged improvised lines with one another on the stage at the St. Mark's Poetry Project. On this particular occasion it was at the suggestion of poet Ron Padgett, as mentioned at the end of the poem.

Line 13: It would appear that Ginsberg incorrectly thought that William Blake's wife's name was Mary, perhaps confusing her with Mary Shelley. In fact William Blake was married to Catherine Sophia Boucher. The editor considered changing the name throughout the poem, but that would give a different syllable count to the lines, so a note will suffice. The form chosen was a ballad and each poet had to improvise alternate rhyming lines in real time in front of an audience.

Line 35: Thomas Stothard (1755–1834) was a British painter and engraver who worked with William Blake.

1980s

Second Spontaneous Collaboration Into the Air, Circa 23 May 1980

Line 5: Arlo Guthrie (b. 1947), Woody Guthrie's son, is also a musician.

Good God I got high bloodpressure answering

More and more frequently Ginsberg's declining health began to creep into his poetry and occupy his mind as the years passed.

Amnesiac Thirst for Fame

Following the murder of John Lennon on December 8, 1980, by a "fan," Ginsberg began to think about the price of fame, something that he had always sought.

A knock, look in the mirror

Following the assassination attempt on President Ronald Reagan on March 30, 1981, Ginsberg asked his class to write a poem about the moment they heard the news. This was Allen's own contribution.

Thundering Undies

In 1981 Ginsberg and Ron Padgett wrote this chain poem together paraphrasing an ode by Catullus in imitation of a poem by Sappho.

Pinsk After Dark

At this time Ted Berrigan was helping to edit Peter Orlovsky's book of poetry entitled *Clean Asshole Poems and Smiling Vegetable Songs*. Berrigan was to die suddenly on July 4, 1983.

Two Scenes

Line 5: The Kiev was one of Ginsberg's favorite all-night diners. Now closed, it once served mushroom barley soup at Second Avenue and 7th Street in New York's East Village.

Listening to Susan Sontag

In 1982 writer Susan Sontag (1933–2004) spoke at Naropa as Ginsberg's guest. Here Allen referenced many specific Boulder sites such as the Chautauqua Meadows and the Flatiron Mountains.

You Want Money?

Ginsberg wrote this poem in response to a preface in a book about obtaining foundation grants.

I used to live in gay sad Paris!

In May 1982 the Dutch artist Karel Appel visited Naropa and collaborated with Ginsberg on several paintings. Allen wrote this poem on one of Appel's canvases.

Having bowed down my forehead on the pavement on Central Park West

Line 2: Ginsberg was once forced to take a cab that was waiting for Chögyam Trungpa.

Back to Wuppertal

Ginsberg wrote this poem and the following one "Am I a Spy from the Moon?" while on an extended reading tour through Europe. Peter Orlovsky was traveling with him and was experiencing severe drug- and alcohol-induced outbursts. Even in the winter snow of Eastern Europe Peter preferred to wear shorts and go barefoot. Steven Taylor was Allen's musical accompanist for the trip and translator Jurgen Schmidt went to several German venues with them.

Line 11: Foulard is a necktie.

Grey clouds hang over

Line 2: The Flatirons were a range of mountains near Boulder, Colorado.

CXXV

This poem was written and titled in the tradition of Ezra Pound's *Cantos.*

Line 2: William Carlos Williams (1883–1963) lived on Ridge Road in Rutherford, New Jersey, when Ginsberg had visited him years earlier.

Line 8: Basil Bunting (1900–1985) was a British poet.

Line 13: Tom Pickard (b. 1946) is a British poet.

Rose Is Gone

Line 12: When Ginsberg was eleven years old he lived with his family in an apartment building at 288 Graham Avenue in Paterson, New Jersey.

Line 24: In 1952–53 Ginsberg lived in an apartment at 206 East 7th Street in New York where he snapped some of his most famous photographs of Kerouac, Burroughs, and Corso.

3'd day down Yangtze River, yesterday

Late in 1984 Ginsberg visited China with a delegation of American writers including Gary Snyder who is mentioned at the end of this poem. When the rest of the writers returned to the Unied States, Allen stayed on to teach until the end of the year.

African Spirituality Will Save the Earth

Near the end of January 1986, Ginsberg returned to Nicaragua at the invitation of poet Ernesto Cardenal (b. 1925). Allen had first visited in 1982 and he was interested to see what had happened to the Nicaraguans' revolutionary spirit in the intervening years.

Bob Dylan Touring with Grateful Dead

Line 10: These and later references to a drunken farmer refer to Peter Orlovsky.

Line 12: Around this time the rents in the East Village began to soar due to gentrification, but Ginsberg was able to keep his rent-controlled apartment for another ten years.

Line 28: Gregory Corso.

1990s

Asia Minor for Gregory

Gregory Corso had a great love for the ancient world, and while Ginsberg was touring Greek ruins in the Aegean with his friend and musical collaborator Philip Glass he wrote this poem for him.

Line 1: Kusadasi was a resort town in Turkey.

Line 8: Bodrum is the contemporary name for the ancient port city Halicarnassus.

The moon in the dewdrop is the real moon

Line 3: Madhyamaka refers to the Mahayana school of Buddhist philosophy.

New Years Greeting

Line 2: Mary Help of Christians Church, torn down in 2013, stood across the street from Ginsberg's apartment on East 12th Street near Avenue A.

Last Conversation with Carl or In Memoriam

On February 26, 1993, a terrorist's bomb exploded in the
garage underneath the World Trade Center. That same day
Ginsberg visited his old friend Carl Solomon (1928–1993) in
the hospital and they watched the television news together.
Allen made notes on their conversation, which he later
arranged into verse. Solomon died on February 26, 1993, and
Ginsberg read this poem at his funeral.

Line 50: Antonin Artaud (1896–1948) was one of
Solomon's favorite French

Line 69: *Neurotica* was a little magazine published by
Jay Landesman (1919–2011) during the early 1950s. Both
Ginsberg and Solomon were contributors.

Notes on the Photographs

1940s. Allen Ginsberg graduated from Eastside High School in Paterson, New Jersey, in 1943 and went on to attend Columbia University. This photograph captures him at his youthful best, eager to experience college life and possibly become a labor lawyer. Before long he would meet Jack Kerouac, William S. Burroughs, and Lucien Carr, and his life would change dramatically. (Page 1) *Photo credit: © Allen Ginsberg LLC*

1950s. On their first trip to Europe in 1957, Ginsberg & Peter Orlovsky stopped in Venice to visit an old friend, Alan Ansen, and took several trips around Italy from there. Here, Ginsberg poses in front of a torso in the Forum in Rome. He and Orlovsky stayed in Venice for a few months before heading on to visit Gregory Corso in Paris. (Page 13) *Photo credit: © Peter Orlovsky*

1960s. After spending nearly a year and a half in India, Ginsberg stopped in Kyoto, Japan, to visit his friends Joanne Kyger and Gary Snyder. There he had his first training in Buddhist meditation with the help of Snyder, before moving on to the Vancouver Poetry Conference in the summer of 1963. (Page 29) *Photo credit: © Gary Snyder*

1970s. In 1973, while visiting Elsa Dorfman at her home in Cambridge, Massachusetts, Ginsberg posed for this picture as he sat on her living room sofa. Allen had known Dorfman since the late fifties when she worked for Grove Press and later, as a well-known photographer, she made numerous portraits of Allen and Peter Orlovsky. (Page 97) *Photo credit: © Elsa Dorfman 2016, All rights reserved.*

1980s. In the fall of 1985, Ginsberg visited Vilnius, Lithuania, as the guest of the Soviet Writers' Union. Allen's mother had been born nearby so the area held a special interest for him. While in his hotel room he snapped this self-portrait in the bathroom mirror. (Page 151) *Photo credit: © Allen Ginsberg LLC*

1990s. In early 1997, Richard Nagler visited Ginsberg in his new loft space above East Fourteenth Street, New York City, where he snapped this photo of him holding his poem "Gone Gone Gone." (Page 193) *Photo credit: © Richard Nagler, 1996, 2016. All rights reserved.*

Index of Titles and First Lines